Cheers to Muses

SANDRA SUNNYO LEE

Yin & Yang. Oil on canvas, diptych, 22" x 24" each

CHEERS TO MUSES

CONTEMPORARY WORKS BY
ASIAN AMERICAN WOMEN

ASIAN AMERICAN WOMEN ARTISTS ASSOCIATION

Library of Congress Control Number: 2006940928

ISBN: 0-9787359-0-0
ISBN: 978-0-9787359-0-6

Cover Art: *Merging.* Clay, 19" x 9" x 8", by Susan Almazol
Title Page Art: Sandra Sunnyo Lee
Cover and Interior Design: Lorraine Rath
Printing and Binding in Malaysia for Imago

For orders, inquiries, and correspondence:
    1890 Bryant Street #302
    San Francisco, CA 94110
    info@aawaa.net
    415-252-7996
Or visit our web site at www.aawaa.net

10 9 8 7 6 5 4 3 2

TABLE OF CONTENTS

ACKNOWLEDGMENTS

AAWAA wishes to thank the following people and organizations for their encouragement, advice, ideas and patience: Patricia Wakida, Amy Lam, Cris Matos, Robert Soto Pla, Natalie Gore, Wei Ming Dariotis, Vanessa Merina, Mark Johnson, Moira Roth, Margo Machida, Sue Tom, Susan Almazol, Intersection for the Arts, Heyday Books, Lenore Chinn, Ruthanne Lum McCunn and Lorraine Rath.

This anthology would not have been possible without the vision of Mary Rose LaFreniere.

Funded in part by the San Francisco Arts Commission, Zellerbach Family Foundation and individual donors.

Asian American Women Artists Association (AAWAA) is excited and pleased to present this mix of contemporary visual and literary art of Asian American women. This anthology focuses equally on both visual and literary artists. The result is a book that presents the reader with a rich view of contemporary life for the Asian American woman and artist across multiple disciplines: visual art of varying media and dimension, fictional and biographical narratives, and poetry.

Over sixty artists and writers, ranging in age from fourteen to eighty-five, and representing a broad spectrum of the Asian Diaspora, are featured in these pages. As our vision for the book was to showcase the diversity of talent among Asian American women, we did not limit the subject matter. You will see images that express both the isolation and integration experienced by Asian American women in American life and society. We invite you to follow their interior journeys through surrealistic landscapes; find symbolic objects that take on lives of their own; read tales that transport you to a reality that is both different and understood; and experience Asian American culture from a multitude of perspectives.

In addition to submitting original works, each contributor was asked to write a dedication to a non-familial Asian American woman whose life or work resonates with the contributor, influencing and inspiring her life, be it her creativity, spirituality, activism or aspiration. Alongside the works throughout the book, the contributors to this anthology cheered muses far and wide. These moving dedications are affirmations to the positive influences these muses have had in their chosen areas of expertise.

Our muses are authentic souls and courageous leaders, often braving the hurdles of criticism or disdain from families, peers and the public in addition to the larger challenges created by social, professional and disciplinary constraints. This unique feature of our anthology distinguishes it from many others and reminds us that we are part of a continuum of the Asian American woman's struggle for equality and creative freedom, both personally and professionally.

Our goal for this anthology is to ask questions that have remained relevant since the first collections of works by Asian American women were published: *Who are these Asian American artists? How easily does Asian American culture integrate the visions of newly arrived Asian artists with the revelations of Asian American women artists who are natives of the United States? What does it mean to be a woman of Asian descent in 21st century America?* The artists in

INTRODUCTION

this anthology respond to these themes and offer fresh perspectives to these questions and many more.

The contributors here continue—and expand—the dialogue begun by their ancestors, many of whom arrived in America more than a century and a half ago. Less obliquely, the contributions here declare that the role of Asian American women artists, writers and poets in their respective communities is a relevant one and one which gives voice to the experiences of Asian American communities. It is a constant exploration as each one seeks, negotiates and defines her artistic journey. The process is not static, and the work of Asian American women artists, writers and poets will continue to require that the natures and conditions of their identities within the Asian American community, as revealed by them in their art and writing, be broadcast loudly and vastly through publications such as *Cheers to Muses*. We hope that this anthology, too, will serve as your muse.

Cheers!

Asian American Women Artists Association
Board of Directors

CHEERS TO MUSES

Cynthia Tom
Dedication

Maya Lin, architect, public art

Maya Lin informs my aspiration to be an outspoken Chinese American in my personal, business and artistic life. At age twenty-one, she won a public design competition for the Vietnam Veterans Memorial and was promptly ridiculed by older, established artists, conservative traditionalists and veterans, and nailed by members of Congress. They wanted to redesign the work to include a traditional statue of soldiers with a flag. She was accused of being a communist. Standing before Congress and during numerous press conferences, she stood her ground with confidence. She demonstrated wisdom, courage and artistic vision as she faced scrutiny, criticism and slander. She has gone on to create many more important Amercian monuments and has become a vital consultant on others.

Cynthia Tom
Location, Location, Location. Acrylics, 40" x 30"

TESSA ZENG
DEDICATION

Zhang Ziyi, actress

I am inspired by the actress Ziyi Zhang, or Zhang Ziyi as she was known to most of us, for only recently she changed her name to the American formatting of putting the first name before the surname. Her breakthrough role was on the film *Crouching Tiger, Hidden Dragon*, and since then she has also starred in the Chinese/American hits *Hero* and *House of Flying Daggers*. Furthermore, she plays the main role in *Memoirs of a Geisha*, which is directed by Steven Spielberg. I admire her greatly for being the first Chinese-born actress to have actually made a place for herself in Hollywood, and to have helped bring Asian culture into the movie industry.

A DIFFERENT WAY
TESSA ZENG

thought winds past our childhood

the swings and sweet sunbeams

as we swim unknowingly through honey—

our liquid staircase to growing up

latching onto a higher, more unbounded, skyscape of time

so we can look back when hands become withered

and wonder at what pulled us up so far

CYNTHIA TOM
Knitting Humanity. Mixed media on canvas, 48" x 36"

LENORE CHINN

Bing. Acrylics, 48" x 66"

BARBARA JANE REYES
DEDICATION

Jessica Hagedorn, performance artist, writer, poet, playwright

Jessica Hagedorn has been my strongest Pilipina literary role model since I was nineteen, which is when I first read her novel *Dogeaters*. Prior to coming across this novel quite accidentally at Cody's Books in Berkeley, I knew of no other Pilipino women in this country who wrote, performed and saw her work published. Were it not for Jessica's visibility, and her sacrilegious, incising, ironic-genre-blending work, it is likely I would not have felt I had the "permission" to pursue writing proactively, on my own terms.

LENORE CHINN
DEDICATION

Bernice Bing, artist

In remembrance of and homage to the late artist Bernice Bing, an early pioneer in the Bay Area's abstract expressionist landscape and a visionary whose commitment to the purity of her art continues to inspire all whose lives she has touched.

SONNET, BECAUSE YOU ASKED ME WHAT SHADES OF ORANGE I SEE
BARBARA JANE REYES

honey tangerine high terror alert

manila mango napalm fire

hibiscus vine climbing rust iron pipe

apricot tree drought stricken mesa

sticky creamsicle melting to slush

unripe cherry poppy shroom

dragonfly trapped in an amber brooch

johnny rotten acid mine drainage

oak leaf in autumn los angeles smog

the planet jupiter coral reef starfish

prison jumpsuit poisonous frog

ballistic missile fuel leak explosion

fifth level of hell where the wrathful burn

151 proof manila bay sunset

NANCY HOM
DEDICATION

Janice Mirikitani, activist, poet

Janice Mirikitani inspires me through her poetry, her passion for justice and her leadership. Besides being an award-winning poet, editor and two-time poet laureate of San Francisco, she is President of the Glide Foundation and Executive Director of Glide's fifty-two programs that provide comprehensive services to the poor, ill and homeless of San Francisco. Her groundbreaking projects have empowered the lives of many people, especially the women and children of the Tenderloin community where Glide is situated. For decades she has been a committed activist, organizing and speaking at numerous marches and rallies. An outspoken supporter of women's rights, she shows by example how women can overcome their feelings of helplessness and define power for themselves. I admire her courage, her tenacity and her humanity.

BAKE SALE DAY
NANCY HOM

It's Bake Sale Day, the school's annual fundraiser, and my daughter wants to bake a pie—a real pie from scratch, not the kind from a box with dehydrated milk and artificial flavors. Nor will she let me buy a cake from Just Desserts and smear the top so it looks homemade. I have run out of excuses. "Everybody's mom bakes," she pleads. "Why don't you ever bake?" "Not everybody's mom bakes," I retort. "Your grandmother, for instance, never baked. She steamed." But Nicole's hand is already deep inside the refrigerator pulling out the butter and eggs.

On Bake Sale mornings, my mother got up extra early before going to the sewing factory to beat together the flour and eggs. I woke to the *phutt phutt* of the hand mixer and the gurgle of boiling water in the wok. She never used the oven. "The gas will blow us to bits like those land mines in Asia," she told us, and stuffed our pots and pans in there instead. The wok hissed and spat. By the time I was dressed, the pale bloated cake was done and waiting for me to take it to school.

Bake Sale Day was the day I hated most in grade school. All of my schoolmates asked their mothers to bake cakes, which we would then sell after school. My mother always made the same kind of cake – a Chinese steamed cake that was spongy and an anemic shade of yellow. It had hardly any sugar, no frosting, no filling, no decorations. It was as plain and bland as the life of a Chinese girl growing up on the Lower East Side, whose after-school social life was counting red convertibles that whizzed beneath the bedroom window. While my classmates were going to birthday parties, my weekends were spent pouring tea for my mother's friends and listening to their gossip as they made dim sum.

"Welllll?" My daughter impatiently taps a spoon on the mixing bowl. "Let's get started." I stare at the two-page recipe and sigh. One third cup of lard, two tablespoons of butter, five eggs, one and a half cups of sugar. I can feel my teeth dissolving one by one. Fat cells in my hips eagerly prepare for company. We use every utensil, every bowl in the house – rolling, mixing, stirring, beating the ingredients into shape. The kitchen becomes a dust cloud of flour and sugar and cream of tartar, which settles on the toaster, frying pan and stove top. We press the lard-laden crust into the pie pan. Lemon juice and egg yolks give the filling a deep yellow hue. We make a meringue frosting of whipped egg whites that foam into massive swirls. Finally we are ready to stick it into the oven.

The other kids could barely contain their snickers when I walked in with my contribution to the sale. Quicky I set the homely cake on the table and surveyed the others with envy. There were cakes with colorful scribbles, sculpted flowers, little diamond chocolates on the sides; cakes with gooey frosting and smiley faces painted on. As usual, mine was the only one left after the bake sale, minus one slice, which a kind teacher always bought. I threw the rest in the garbage can on the way back from school.

"Did everyone like the cake?" my mother asked in her broken English. "Yes," I lied, and watched her beam. "Chinese steamed cake is the best—light, fluffy, not too sweet, not too fancy; a modest simple cake—I knew everyone would like it." I ran to my room and slammed the door. She didn't understand. She didn't have to go to school and face a room full of blond and red-haired kids whose mothers joined the PTA and wore dresses from Bloomingdale's. She didn't have to stand before them, a shy quiet Chinese girl with a meek little cake that nobody wanted. I swore I would never bake anything when I grew up.

Nicole and I count each minute and stare at the oven.

Before the timer rings, we open the door and pull the pie out. The crust is burnt a little on the edge but the meringue stands proud and stiff like the snowy peaks of Kilimanjaro. Nicole is pleased. "It looks just like the picture in the recipe book! You're the best, Mom." I am relieved. This pie will pass the test, I'm sure. There will be more than one slice eaten; it can hold its own among the other cakes and pies at school.

I myself have grown fond of plain cakes without much sugar and without any frosting – light fluffy cakes in a very becoming shade of maize. They have a delicate flavor and fragrance unlike other cakes. I asked my mother for the recipe. "Why Chinese steamed cake? You always preferred the sticky heavy kind." "I'm starting to appreciate the simplicity of your cakes," I answered. "I feel good when I eat them."

The next time Nicole and I bake, I take out the Chinese steamed cake recipe, but she crinkles her nose. She wants to bake the strawberry and kiwi cheesecake fruit tart in the Martha Stewart magazine. I neatly fold my mother's recipe and put it in a special drawer. One day she will ask for it and it will be there.

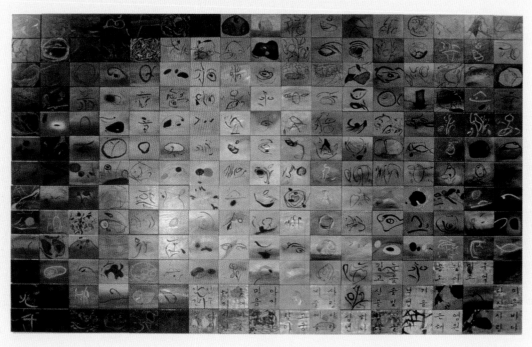

KAY KANG

A picture is…a thousand words. 221 wood blocks
each 5.5" x 7", oil and wood, 72" x 122"

Kay Kang
Dedication

Maya Lin, artist, architect

Maya Lin has designed several of the most significant and best known works of public art of the late 20th century. As a twenty-one-year-old undergraduate student of architecture at Yale, she won the 1981 commission to design the Vietnam Veterans Memorial in Washington D.C. The Vietnam War memorial is a very powerfully evocative and minimalist monument. She also designed the Civil Rights Memorial in Montgomery, Alabama, the Women's Table at Yale University and many other amazing and influential architectural projects. Lin has created environments capable of moving visitors to great emotion. At one point, she said, "An artist struggles to retain the integrity of work so that it remains a strong, clear vision." Her life and arts have been deep inspirations for me.

Kay Kang

It's a Girl!! Installation: acrylics, charcoal, hemp rope, peppers, door jam, 82" x 55" x 70"

ZOHRA SAED

DEDICATION

Meena Alexander, poet, scholar

This piece is dedicated to Meena Alexander, poet and scholar, who taught me that remembering is a revolutionary act. I was nineteen years old when I read her memoir *Fault Lines* and I was struck by the power of her voice. It was also the first time I had read of a woman writer who carried multiple worlds and languages within her and was able to make sense of these complexities through writing. When I was twenty-two I met her for an interview and she was kind enough to welcome me into her home. I sat on her couch and told her how difficult I felt being transplanted so many times and having so many languages jostle in my head. She comforted me by saying that these fragments were the very things that would give me strength to write. Years have passed and I am still under her tutelage as a doctoral student. My writing blossomed because of the strength I found in her guidance.

MARCH 11, 1981
A SIX-YEAR-OLD BIRTHDAY PARTY

ZOHRA SAED

Sheepshead Bay, Brooklyn

One velvet rug nailed to the wall of our dining room, purchased in Mecca, Saudi Arabia. Was it pre- or post-Hajj? I don't remember. I snuggle my nose into the fabric and sniff deep enough to smell the incense from the bazaars of Mecca. It consoles the separation anxiety I feel from where I consider home: Saudi Arabia. Although, it is a different experience for my father, who fled the country because of the discrimination we faced there as Afghan refugees.

When I start kindergarten at PS 254, I am known as the little Arab girl. My teachers think we are wealthy Arabs from the Gulf. Ms. Sokoloff puts away my 22-karat necklace, earrings and two baby girl bangles to keep them safe. They are never returned. I don't know how to ask for them back. No one seems to know that we are from Afghanistan. No one is confused that I look more Chinese than Arab. I am the rich little Arab girl. Ms. Sokoloff gives my father a shopping list of things we need for kindergarten parties: napkins, plastic utensils, plates, crayons…enough for the entire class. My father buys them all from our savings.

One atlas of the world framed and placed next to the velvet rug with the image of Mecca. I stand on a chair as my father traces the trajectory of our voyage from Afghanistan, to Iran, to Jordan, to Saudi Arabia and then to the United States. I learn the names of these cities before the names of my grandparents. Sometimes, we stand there for hours as my father tells me stories of our ancestors. I ask if I can pin a little red flag on the city where I was born, Jalalabad, Afghanistan, and a green flag on the city where my brother was born, Riyadh, Saudi Arabia. I settle for tracing the steps between our cities with my fingers. We are named after the stars of the place we are born in: 1975, Zohra after the morning star (visible as my father delivered me) and 1979, Sharif after Omar Sharif.

One dental degree from International School of Dentistry, Lahore, Pakistan, 1969. A golden seal. My father, a handsome, dashing young man, returns home to continue a long generation of dentists from his paternal line in Jalalabad. In the army, stationed in Ghazni, he serves as the army dentist. After his mandatory army training, he travels to Eastern and Northern Afghanistan for two years to serve the villages with no modern dentists, only barbers who also pull teeth on the side of the street. In America, this gold-framed degree opens some doors for my father, but not all. It is this "not all" part that has him working at gas stations until we understand the nature of keys and doors in this country.

My father, in tuxedo and dark-rimmed glasses, celebrates my birthday in high style. I have my hair curled with hot rollers because I want my hair to look like Wonder Woman's hair. She is the American woman I fall in love with at the age of five and I am devoted to her show which comes on everyday at 5pm on Channel 5. I twirl around the house and bang my head into walls trying to be her. I am dressed in Eid clothes. It is a brand new blue velvet dress with a frilly white skirt. My brother is dressed up in new clothes as well and has his hair neatly combed to the side. His pacifier hangs from his neck on a little chain that my father made for him.

We are running out of money. My parents eat farina almost everyday, while my brother and I get some soup with some meat and carrots. There are no job prospects for my father. He has to return to school. Birthday cakes are expensive. We no longer lived in the luxury of our past. But my father doesn't care. He says, "Leave it to God, he will find an answer for us."

This is my first birthday in America and it is the happiest day in the world. I am a princess still, even though I punch my classmates for not understanding me. My heart is constricted; my father says, "diltangeh." I try and try before I become violent. I speak to them in Arabic, then Dari and then finally Uzbeki, but they don't understand any of it. So I throw a tantrum, punch or push them and then climb to the top of the playhouse to sit on the roof till playtime is over. The teacher sends me home with a letter and a phone call about my bad behavior. But it doesn't matter to my father. He says, it is good for a girl to have some spunk. The only change is that my nickname shifts from Ipek kiz, silk thread daughter, to a simple shortening of my name to Zor, strength. I still get pink roses on my cake just like I asked.

The baker writes my name in English as they have misspelled it in my official papers, Zahera. In America, Zohra is only the name my family and Afghan friends call me. Zahera, pronounced like the desert with a "Z," is what the teachers and kids call out to me in school. The baker adds an extra year for good luck, so my cake says that I am seven years old. My cake says that "Zahera" is seven years old. I barely recognize who I am here. Father wraps up the kitchen knife with a yellow ribbon. There are no balloons. But it's okay, I hate balloons because I am so afraid of them popping and it irritates me to see wilting old balloons. There are no other kids at this party. But it's okay, I hate the other kids and I've beaten most of them. There is only us and this is enough.

I feed my father the first bite out of the first slice of my birthday cake. This is my happiest day in America. It is the only day I do not sniff the edges of my velvet rug to smell Saudi Arabia and remember my playroom with the indoor swing and rows of cars, robots, airplanes, horses and Legos that made my friends jealous.

GENNY LIM
DEDICATION

Yuri Kochiyama, activist

The Asian American woman who I most admire and consider a positive role model to me is Yuri Kochiyama. She is a remarkable woman who embodies the qualities of a loving mother, friend, cultural worker, political activist and fearless leader. I have never known her to compromise her social values or her hands-on community grassroots approach to progressive social change in all the years that she has lent her name, her formidable energy and her physical body to countless causes against oppression and injustice. Her arena of focus expands beyond the borders of the Asian American community into all countries, ethnicities and cultures. She was way ahead of her time in her youth and she remains ahead of her time in her cronehood.

ANNUNCIATION
GENNY LIM

What has visited me?

The great gray spectre of Market Street?

Grandma *Kwan Yin* has taken my seat on the 30 Stockton

Weighed down with kosher chickens, cut scallions and

The nine ingredients of health and prosperity

She will dole out lucky red envelopes with gold embossed

Double-happiness blessings to all the fat buddha babies of Chinatown

But can she fill the shriveled stomach of homelessness?

And where will all the plastic bags of tomorrow go?

Will they hold enough food for the dying?

Will they hold enough compassion to cool

The angry heels of American youth?

You must believe in karma

Because as luck would have it

All the chickens have come home to roost

And dust enshrouds the Cathedral Mall

Where paper gods preach their colonial gospel and

Cash registers syncopate the Dow industrial mantra

Two-and-a-half points up!

Standard & Poor's, *Three-and-eight-quarters down!*

What will the Angel of Mercy bring to celebrate?

One-thousand-year-old lotus eggs preserved in mud?

The food of the gods have long been regurgitated

There will be no more banquets this year

The haves have and the have nots have nothing

but the crumbs of promises and

together they will be sitting at the table

to eat

to eat

NAOKO HARUTA DEDICATION

NAOKO HARUTA
Life #15. Acrylics, 43" x 67"

Haruko Obata, flower arranger

Haruko Obata came to San Francisco from Fukuoka, Japan around 1910, and a few years later married Chiura Obata, a Japanese painter who would go on to develop his own unique style of Sumi-e, Japanese ink and brush painting. Soon thereafter she introduced the art of Japanese flower arrangement in the United States. She gave demonstrations and taught classes of her art for more than seven decades. She transformed a few simple flowers into a work of art. In her arrangements each and every flower sang, showing off its own unique beauty. She knew how to capture the essence of each flower. Her art, her spirited personality and her expansive generosity touched many lives. I am fortunate to have been one of them.

LORI KAY
DEDICATION

Ruth Asawa, sculptor, artist

Ruth Asawa has been an influential role model in my career for two decades. She is an outstanding artist and art activist who combines her career with her family life. I have great respect for her work and am in awe of her public art. Ms. Asawa, based in San Francisco, has successfully cleared a path for other women in art advocacy, public art and sculpture. For more than five decades, Ms. Asawa has been associated with some of the most notable figures in American twentieth century art. As an art student, after years in a Japanese internment camp, she studied at the legendary Black Mountain College under Josef Albers and Buckminster Fuller, alongside John Cage, Merce Cunningham, Robert Rauschenberg and Jasper Johns. A vocal advocate in the arts, Ms. Asawa has produced an impressive body of work, well loved public art and taught children's art.

LORI KAY
Hat. Bronze, 20" x 16" x 16"

M. GRACE ILAGAN ANGEL
DEDICATION

Jessica Hagedorn, performance artist, writer, poet, playwright

The moment I entered the café in the Mission where a skinny woman with a pixie haircut was speaking in front of a very colorful audience, I felt right at home. Her voice and words were as familiar to me as my own. She spoke of places and people, of scents and colors, of love and loss. She spoke of home. Home, where I was born in the Philippines. Home, where I came of age here in the U.S. There is a Filipino saying, "Pinay parin," literally meaning, "Still a Filipino." Jessica Hagedorn was born and raised in the Philippines. An immigrant like myself questioning our place, swimming for identity. A Filipino in America? Hagedorn writes, "What does this new-found identity mean? The longing for what was precious and left behind in the Philippines begins to creep in and take over my work." Hagedorn is a writer tagged twice but it will always be about the language, "the dreams in secret languages." So it is to her I dedicate this poem, a souvenir from home.

DROUGHT
M. GRACE ILAGAN ANGEL

He smoothed the wrinkles on my belly
And sucked my bitter fruit
We ploughed an ocean in my navel
And sowed mountains of regret into fields
We sank our roots deeper into the dirt and
Allowed only the memory of water
To sustain our thirst
We dreamt of rain
And quietly
Listened for our trees to bear fruit

LORI KAY
Chair in Motion. Bronze, 10'4" x 2'6" x 8'

KEIKO NELSON

Birth=Wave. Sand and clay scuplture, mixed media
painting on canvas, 800 sq. ft. installation

Keiko Nelson
Dedication

Ruth Asawa, sculptor, artist

In the mid-70s, I met Ruth Asawa, an extraordinary sculptor who for over three decades has had many solo exhibits of sculpture, drawings and lithographs. Her background, like mine, is Japanese. She combined her career as an artist with being the mother of six children. Ruth was a driving force in the development of art programs in San Francisco public schools.

When I had my first baby, Ruth encouraged my art; when I was divorced, she encouraged my art again. She inspires my life as an artist. Ruth's philosophy of making art is "There is no separation between studying, performing the daily chores of living and creating one's own work." I have the same Zen Buddhist philosophy as Ruth.

Keiko Nelson
Echoes Through Time. 3-D mixed-media sculpture, 400 sq. ft. installation

ROSHNI RUSTOMJI

DEDICATION

Mirrha/Catarina de San Juan, slave, visionary

A young girl named Mirrha (most probably an abbreviation of Maryam because she said her name meant amurga, bitterness) was abducted from India in about 1618 by Portuguese pirates and was baptized Catarina de San Juan by the Jesuit priests in Cochin, India before being brought to New Spain in 1621 as a slave on the Manila Galleon. She died in Puebla in 1688. Merely a sketch of the story of her long life appears in the story I have titled, "The Gift of Chocolate." Two contemporary biographies of her were written by two of her father confessors and although they are slanted because they were written to support their offering of Mirrha-Catarina's name for canonization, a vivid portrait of Mirrha-Catarina as an amazing woman emerges from these pages. To many people, Mirrha-Catarina is a gentle, pious and humble visionary, even a Beata. To me she is an extraordinary woman who combined compassion with strength. I consider Mirrha-Catarina as one of my ancestors in the Americas. She has taught me invaluable lessons about survival, about strength and about compassion. In dedicating this story to Mirrha-Catarina, I am also expressing my gratitude to the many women from Asia whose names I don't know, who arrived in the Americas through the centuries, often brought here without their consent and too often because they were forced to leave their homes in Asia. To the women from Asia who lived, worked, grew old and died in these lands, the women who have made it easier for me to call the Americas my home, a brief narrative about a woman from Asia.

THE GIFT OF CHOCOLATE

ROSHNI RUSTOMJI

The store at the corner of Calle Alianza and Calzado de la Republica in Oaxaca had a bright green sign over the door. Elegantly painted with what looked like a pattern of dragons and birds, it boldly proclaimed in bright red letters the name of the store: SIN NOMBRE. The owner of this store named NAMELESS was known as Maestra Sofia throughout Oaxaca and although she sold the usual things that small stores sell across the United States of Mexico—bread and tortillas and refrescos and milk and small packages of cookies and crackers and potato chips and some sandwiches, some cheese, some fruits—Maestra's store was best known for the chocolate she sold.

My first visit to SIN NOMBRE was to buy Maestra's homemade, individually wrapped pieces of dark brown chocolate speckled with sugar and cinnamon. It was chocolate that could be eaten or drunk for the mere pleasure of its taste or for its healing powers. As I picked up five packets of almond-flavored chocolate, I told Maestra that I needed to be fortified by either countless cups of black tea or numerous mugs of chocolate—both hot, both very sweet—throughout the day and into the night as I worked on my project on Catarina de San Juan of Puebla de los Angeles. Maestra Sofia knew about Catarina de San Juan who was abducted from India and brought to Puebla, New Spain as a slave in 1621. Oh yes, she said, she knew about Catarina's piety and visions and her skill as a healer and an exorcist. She also knew how at her death, the name of this slave and servant was offered for canonization. Maestra wasn't pleased with the Holy Office, the Inquisition's harsh denial of the submission of Catarina's name for sainthood. Maestra's comments led us into a discussion about how history mutates into legends and how instead of sainthood, a fantasized history was woven around Catarina many years after her death. We talked about the fantastic history that transformed Mirrha-Catarina into a Chinese princess and the first, the "ur" China Poblana. A China Poblana of the wonderful bright skirts, blouses, rebosos and distinctive dances. We spoke about how Catarina de San Juan, renowned for covering her beauty with drab robes, her face always hidden within a hood, was turned into a colorful, flamboyant symbol of Mexico. How the woman who spoke about her terror of men was made into the female counterpart of the charro. Maestra Sofia and I marveled at the ways of the world and her historians.

I told Maestra Sofia that I had spent the afternoon reading about the extraordinary, magical chocolate-making ability of Catarina. An ability that the citizens of seventeenth century Puebla had exploited even when Catarina, aged, partially blind and paralyzed throughout the left side of her body, was facing death. It was a skill that was profitable to the citizens. In whatever quantity they brought the ingredients to Catarina—the raw chocolate, the sugar, the cinnamon, the almonds, definitely some vanilla, very often some dried, dark red chilies—to be made into chocolate that could be eaten, drunk or cooked, the quantities increased under the miraculous healing hands of the pious woman who spoke to Jesus, the Virgin and the saints, and prayed while darning stockings and preparing chocolate. The final product she handed over to her clients exceeded their expectations. Not only in quantity but in quality. Quite a few of her clients praised her. Many of them used her services while despising her as a slave-turned-servant who was born in a heathen, uncivilized land. Of course no one paid the woman living and dying in poverty extra money for the extra chocolate they received.

Maestra Sofia said, "Yes, chocolate. Such history. Such stories. What about that Bishop of Chiapas who died when he drank a cup of hot chocolate prepared by some of the highborn ladies of his congregation? It happened about the same time as Catarina was being buried in Puebla." Since I had not heard this particular chocolate story and since no one was trying to buy anything at SIN NOMBRE at that particular time, Maestra Sofia invited me to sit down next to her on the high bench behind the counter while she told me the story about the Bishop of Chiapas and chocolate.

Apparently the Bishop of Chiapas had forbidden the ladies of his congregation to bring all the paraphernalia of making hot chocolate to church. The braziers, the chocolate, the milk or the water, the cups, all of these carried into the church by the ladies' servants and slaves in order to make hot, frothy chocolate for their mistresses were forbid-

den. The ladies felt that, denied this exotic, newly discovered drink, they would not be able to survive the familiar old world rituals in this strange new land of accessible chocolate and elusive gold. Maestra Sofia said that those ladies would have been aware that the Bishop knew that chocolate was supposedly an aphrodisiac.

"I don't know if the ladies believed this but the Bishop seemed to have believed in the aphrodisiac temptation of chocolate." Said Maestra Sofia, "He wanted no secularly aroused ladies in his congregation. Or maybe the preparation and the drinking of the chocolate interfered with his delivery and the ladies' appreciation of his sermons. Anyway, the Bishop forbade chocolate. At least in the church. So the ladies took their revenge and made room for a new Bishop. One of the ladies invited the offending Bishop for a cup of afternoon chocolate at her home that was quite far from the church. She offered him a cup of chocolate that she had poisoned with the help and blessings of the other ladies. It was done with such finesse and skill that no one could prove the lady's guilt. And no one asked what the Bishop was doing, drinking this forbidden heathen drink with the ladies of his congregation." But rumors about the cause of the Bishop's death, according to Maestra Sofia, persist to this day throughout Latin America.

I, named Jahanara Mody by my parents, have always held a strong belief in the beneficial powers of chocolate and I know that it should never be withheld from anyone. To prove my point, I told Maestra Sofia the following story about my paternal grandmother and the miracle of chocolate. It was September 1947, a month after the birth of Pakistan. My father and I were coming home from Thackery's Bookshop when we saw a man and his daughter huddled under the street lamp on the sidewalk in front of our house. I had seen them earlier among the refugees from India trying to find some kind of shelter in Karachi, this new capital city of the new country of

Pakistan. The little girl looked very tired and was crying for her mother. When we told my grandmother about them, she invited them into the house. My mother gave them food. The girl would eat nothing. She looked at everyone with eyes that were scared and dazed and pleading. All she would say was, "Where is my Ammi?" The man whispered to Bapaiji, "Her mother is dead. Killed. She saw it all. The attack. The slaughter. She was hiding behind a door."

Bapaiji started praying softly while she walked to the cabinet where she kept her prayer books. She opened the cabinet and pulled out two bars of dark, bittersweet chocolate. I knew very well that the chocolate hadn't been there earlier because I kept my schoolbooks in the same cabinet and I had checked that very same cabinet for a missing notebook the previous hour. I also knew that our family couldn't afford that kind of chocolate. I had often heard whispers and murmurs about my grandmother's "powers." I had heard that whenever she was faced with any kind of disaster or whenever she saw a hungry person, my grandmother could somehow find or create food. This was the first time I had seen my grandmother's "powers" in action and it seemed special to me because it involved chocolate. Expensive English chocolate.

Grandmother sat the little girl on her lap and coaxed her into eating one whole bar of chocolate. She said that chocolates, religion and politics were all "melted together" in her mind. She rocked the little girl to sleep in her lap and reminisced. "My parents used to send me to a lady from England who lived far from our house. I went for my classes twice every week. They wanted me to learn English. As one of my rather timid and not very intelligent aunties used to say, 'The English—they were so clever! Even their little children speak English!' My English teacher was very strict. She never smiled. She was a good teacher but she always gave me strange presents when I had done well at my lessons. Pictures of Jesus Christ as a baby, as a young man, as a man dying across two pieces of wood. She also gave me pictures of British kings and queens and princes and princesses. After a year of tutoring me, she decided to return to what she called her 'civilized home.' After my last class, she gave me a big box of chocolates, hugged me and began to cry. 'How sad,' she said. 'How very, very sad. You are such a sweet girl. You are so intelligent. But oh my, oh my, after you are dead you will burn in hell for eternity because you are still a heathen. All those cards and pictures I sent with you to your home. Nothing happened. I will pray for you. You poor, poor child.' I thanked my teacher for the chocolates. She asked me to thank her for her prayers and I did so. The chocolates were delicious."

I told Maestra Sofia that I had nearly forgotten my grandmother's story. I didn't know if I had believed that the chocolate she fed that little girl was really real chocolate until earlier that afternoon when I read about Catarina de San Juan and chocolate before coming to SIN NOMBRE.

Maestra Sofia said that she knew a couple of women with the same kind of food-producing powers and as for Catarina, "I can tell you all kinds of stories about Catarina de San Juan. Stories that you won't find in any of the books you are reading. Family stories. I am the only living descendant of one of the two sons Catarina's husband, the Chinese slave Domingo Suarez, had with another woman when Catarina refused to consummate her marriage with him. Because she had promised herself to Christ."

"I don't think Christ had all that much to do with it," I said. "She was scared of men. One can't forget that she had been raped and abused when she was kidnapped." I was trying to deal with Catarina de San Juan's never-ending words of praise and gratitude for the Spanish and Portuguese Jesuits who had baptized her after she had been kidnapped by a boatload of Portuguese pirates. Her constant praise of those who had "saved" her from hellfire and damnation was difficult for me to understand. A fiercely nationalistic family had after all, brought me up

in the days of the successful struggle of India for Independence from the British. Soft-spoken Maestra Sofia raised her voice. She was trembling, "Who would want anything to do with sex after what that poor child went through? She punished herself throughout her life. Flagellating herself even when she was barely a young woman. A teenager. Starving herself. The woman who came to prepare her for her burial, to bathe and dress her, wept at the sight of the terrible wounds and scars that covered that frail, small woman's body."

I saw tears in Maestra Sofia's eyes and invited her to my house for lunch. I needed to hear stories about Catarina de San Juan from a woman. The books about her I was reading were by men. Men intent on sanctifying her, explaining her, analyzing her. I wondered if Maestra Sofia knew anything about Catarina's death. Did Catarina de San Juan speak of the land of her birth as she lay dying? Did she remember the sound of her mother's voice calling her by the name she had given her longed-for daughter at her birth, Maryam, whom she affectionately called Mirrha? Kidnapped, raped, her name stripped from her, taught to believe her sufferings were part of her salvation, her glorious martyrdom; did Mirrha hear her mother's voice calling her as she was dying?

NELLIE WONG
DEDICATION

Suey Ting Gee, waitress/cook

To Suey Ting Gee, whose peasant tenacity loomed forth from a small village in Toishan to Oakland's Chinatown where I was born, whose strength was not always visible to the searching eye, and whose dreams, tough love and elbow grease raised an American family.

KATHERINE WESTERHOUT
DEDICATION

Maya Lin, architect, artist

Maya Lin, well known as the creator of the Vietnam Veterans Memorial and the Southern Poverty Law Center Civil Rights Memorial, has said, "I cannot remember a time when…I did not feel humbled by the beauty of the natural world. I take inspiration from… natural phenomena." Her connection to the natural world and her ability to transmit its essence to others is the source of her brilliance; and beauty is always there, not as a sentiment, but inseparable from the power of her work. As a photographer whose subjects derive exclusively from natural phenomena, I am greatly inspired by Maya Lin, by the consistent power of her work to communicate at the deepest levels of our consciousness, her commitment to excellence in its execution, and the grace of both her work and her public presence, which tower above the fray as the embodiment of Eastern sensibility and the female principle.

PANTOUM FOR PANCAKES
NELLIE WONG

A Chinese woman in America made the best pancakes ever
Not Betty Crocker, not Julia Child, you know?
With a Chinese soupspoon in hand, such fervor
She heaped 7 soupspoons of flour just so

Not Betty Crocker, not Julia Child, you know?
She measured two cups of milk with precision
And 4 drops of egg color into a bowl
A couple of shakes of salt without derision

She measured two cups of milk with precision
Added 3 soupspoons sugar, 2 teaspoons baking powder
A couple of shakes of salt without derision
With Ma's pancakes who'd want clam chowder?

Added 3 soupspoons sugar, 2 teaspoons baking powder
Stir up a storm, plopped in another soupspoon of flour
With Ma's pancakes who'd want clam chowder?
Customers at the Great China succumbed to her power

Stir up a storm, plopped in another soupspoon of flour
A ritual of love and survival wielded this woman with care
Customers at the Great China succumbed to her power
Waiting with knives and forks in working hands bare

A ritual of love and survival wielded this woman with care
Feeding pensioner, salesmen and bachelors together
Waiting with knives and forks in working hands bare
During World War II in all kinds of weather

Feeding pensioner, salesmen and bachelors together

No longer a village woman waiting for money, nothing to sell

Waitress and cook, no time to learn and play a zither

Learning English from us children and radio she would excel

No longer a village woman waiting for money, nothing to sell

With a Chinese soupspoon in hand, such fervor

Learning English from us children and radio she would excel

A Chinese woman in America made the best pancakes ever

KATHERINE WESTERHOUT
Richmond VII. Photographic image printed with archival
pigmented inks on rag paper

SUSAN ALMAZOL
DEDICATION

Chitra Bannerjee Divakaruni, writer

The clarity and magic of Chitra Bannerjee Divakaruni's writing strengthens my resolve to tell my truth in the complex ways I have lived it, growing up as I did in three countries: the Philippines, Japan and the United States. The cultural richness of her stories also inspires me to share the cultural complexity of my own life, including being raised as a Filipina, marrying an African American and raising a bicultural daughter. I am also profoundly grateful to Chitra for the delightful surprise of finding my own special secrets, the powerful "calling thought," described in *The Mistress of Spices*.

SUSAN ALMAZOL
Merging. Clay, 19" x 9" x 8"

MARY CHI-WHI KIM
DEDICATION

Janice Mirikitani, poet

Janice Mirikitani, author of the collection of poems entitled *Shedding Silence*, first awakened me to the power of poetry to speak to our realities as Asian American women; through activism and multimedia arts, Janice has gone on to serve our communities, both Asian American and the larger one, in very strategic ways. She is among my many literary inspirations, including AI, Marilyn Chin, Cathy Song, Maxine Hong Kingston and Ishle Park.

SEAWEED DIVERS
MARY CHI-WHI KIM

Black-green ribbons soaked in the kitchen sink.
They wavered and curled, grazing stainless steel.
Planted on the counter by Mother, I dipped
Bare arms into *miyuk*, imagined slick fishes,

A whole school, tickling my wrists.
"Little one, stop bathing in our supper."
Mother rinsed and sautéed sea greens,
Added water, sesame to simmer *miyukgook*.

She cooled and spooned broth in my mouth.
"When you still suckled my breast, my *umah*
Made me eat *miyukgook*. Your turn now."
I opened up as she lowered a strand,

Savory like scallion, chewy like noodles.
"Your daddy loves it. His favorite cousin's
A *hae nyuh* who dives into the sea for *miyuk*.
Eat more before our bath."

Blue-black strands set loose on foam,
Mother's hair tickled my shoulders.
I plied her hair atop my head, plunged
To salvage a strand, and started chewing.

CHRISTINA MAZZA
DEDICATION

Nancy Kwan, actress

When I was in my early 20s, I saw the movie *The World of Suzie Wong* and was struck by the leading actress, Nancy Kwan. I was impressed by the inner strength of the character she portrayed as well as her outer beauty. Since I was adopted at birth by white parents, Nancy Kwan was the first Eurasian face I had seen other than my own up to that point in my life. It was this movie and this wonderful actress from Hong Kong that inspired me to look into my own Asian identity and subsequently into discovering my own inner strength and talents.

ELIZABETH GORDON
DEDICATION

Phan Thi Kim Phuc, peace activist

Phan Thi Kim Phuc and I were born a year apart in South Vietnam. In the summer of 1972, while I played tag in a safe American subdivision and only ran shrieking when the Sno-Cone truck made its tinkling appearance, Kim Phuc ran screaming from a napalm bomb attack on her village. The photograph of Kim—burned, naked, fleeing in terror—has become one of the iconic images of the Vietnam War. But it is Kim the flesh-and-blood woman, not the iconic child, whom I honor. Having survived her injuries, she spends her adult life speaking out for peace. Not only is she a living reminder of all that my countrymen, both Vietnamese and American, have suffered, but the wounds permanently seared on her body symbolize the scars, visible and invisible, borne by all of us whose lives have been altered by the peculiar hatred we call war.

TESTIFY
ELIZABETH GORDON

When they came to my door I don't know who they are. I see clean white shirt, stripe tie, black pants. Long pants, even though summer so hot. I say *who you want* and they say they come talk to me. I say *okay* and step outside on the porch. The sun is go down. I see my neighbor hurry finish mow his grass. In the air strong smell of gasoline and sweet smell of grass just been cut. They ask if I know Jesus and now in their hands I see many papers and books with pages edge gold. They act so serious. They hold book to their heart and tell how Jesus die for me, Jesus suffer terrible, and when I laugh they all look so surprise. Their eyes go huge like moon, and I say *I hear many*

CHRISTINA MAZZA
Poppies. Pen & ink with gouache, 14" x 9"

times abut Jesus suffer and *I know what crucify mean.* And they say very good and ask if I am save. When I laugh at them more they act so funny, so I show them my arm *see here is where I burn* and my feet and leg *see here is where I cut.* I pull my hair back and show them *here my ear is gone* because it take for souvenir. Then everything quiet. My neighbor finish mow and sky get dark. I tell them *go now,* but one is so stubborn he try to give me book, try push book in door when I am go back inside. When I tell him *stop* he ask don't you believe in God? And I think stupid boy I just show you God don't believe in me.

LISA CHIU
DEDICATION

Maya Lin, architect, artist

I first learned about artist/architect Maya Lin when I was eleven, while scanning a Cleveland newspaper for a story to report for my classroom's News Day. Up until then, News Day was a dreaded weekly occurrence. But then I found the story of the Asian American college student who won a blind competition—against more than 1,000 entrants—to design the Vietnam Veterans Memorial. Like me, Maya Lin was an Ohio-raised Asian American young woman. I was excited to report the news to my class. That story stayed with me and even influenced me in my career choice. Ever since that fifth grade News Day, I've developed a passion for journalism and for sharing important stories. To this day, Maya Lin inspires me in exemplifying strength, grace, integrity and clear vision.

PEARL BALLS OF WISDOM
LISA CHIU

Maybe it's petty of me, but I decided upon a litmus test to determine whether or not I'll like someone. It all hinges on if a person will eat my rice pearl balls, my signature potluck dish.

What's not to like about my beloved pearl balls? They may look like porcupine meatballs, but the sticky rice exterior belies a heavenly combination of ground pork, ginger, scallions, water chestnuts, soy sauce and sesame oil. Quite simply, they are tasty orbs of perfection.

Recently, I offered my pearl balls at a neighborhood block party. My fuzzy spheres looked ridiculously out of place next to three potato salads, two pasta salads, a tray of deviled eggs, a platter of hot dogs and a few plates of chocolate chip cookies. I had some explaining to do, I could tell. "They're basically Chinese meatballs," I said. Thankfully, the pearl balls were devoured. What a relief—my neighbors passed my test.

For a moment, though, I was worried. Potlucks with strangers are much like the first day of kindergarten. Instead of wondering if anyone will like me, now I dread the possibility of no one touching my dish. Just as I was shy as a child, I'm timid as a cook. At age thirty-five, I can count on one hand the number of times I've hosted meals I've cooked myself.

In my single years when I lived in tiny apartments that counted a hot plate as a kitchen, I used to be the type who always brought store-bought sweets to potlucks. But as I got older and my kitchen space increased, I found that potlucks gave me a reason to build my culinary skills. Each time the invitation came, I'd run through possible ideas, scour cookbooks and pester friends for advice. After I got over the initial anxiety and finally whipped something together, I'd eventually look forward to the meal with great anticipation, where a glorious bounty of dishes awaited.

Health experts today say it's dangerous to link food with emotion, but those people can't possibly be Asian. The potlucks of my childhood bring back rich, wonderful memories. Those cherished meals offered an unlikely mix of foods that would only make sense at a Taiwanese American Thanksgiving dinner in Cleveland. Alongside Judy's Special Salad and Maggie's Potato Mushroom Casserole were my mom's Bean Thread Noodles, Jen's mom's Sticky Rice, and of course, a big roasted turkey with stuffing.

My fascination with potlucks hasn't waned over the years; if anything, I'm more obsessed with them than ever. If it weren't for potlucks, I wouldn't have learned that thinly sliced radishes provide a delightful addition to a pasta salad. I'd have never thought to combine Jell-O, whipped cream and pretzels as a sweet/salty, soft/crunchy dessert. It never would have occurred to me to combine crunchy peanut butter, sesame oil, and pasta to make a delicious nutty noodle dish.

More important than helping me expand my recipe repertoire, though, potlucks force me to define myself. What can I cook that really represents me? It took some time for me to settle on pearl balls as my signature dish. First, I went through a long phase of baking brownies and cupcakes. The first time I prepared pearl balls for anyone was for an all-Asian group of twenty-somethings in Los Angeles. They were a hit. Buoyed by my success, I made them for a multigenerational Asian American Thanksgiving gathering in San Jose. Success again!

Since moving back to Ohio recently, I've noticed that my pearl balls are often regarded with curious suspicion at first. Even though Chinese food is common pretty much everywhere in the United States, pearl balls generally aren't offered in Chinese restaurants. That's part of what makes them special to me.

Since I'm living in a place where Asians are few in number, I always have a twinge of doubt when facing a potluck invitation. Dare I offer my delectable pearl balls? Is that too ethnic for this crowd? Maybe I should offer something standard, something more familiar. I could prepare egg rolls, but that's obvious—and I won't even eat those myself. No, if you want to know me, you need to know that I'm much like my savory pearl balls, accessible but distinctive. Plus, pearls go with everything.

This week, I'm preparing my pearls for two family events. It doesn't matter to me that one crowd is wine and cheese and the other peanut butter and jelly. I'm curious to see what everyone else will bring to these occasions. In this beer-guzzling, football-loving city I live in, the kind of beer you drink says a lot about you. The same can be said for what you bring to a potluck. Potlucks offer a clear view into the soul of the dish-bearer. What, literally, do you bring to the table?

MACHIKO KONDO
DEDICATION

Yoko Ono, performance artist

When I saw some of Yoko Ono's Instruction Pieces, her paintings brought a new visual meaning and conceptual essence into my work. It was a terrible sensation and my heart started pounding. Next, I was sent into the memory of my childhood: I liked to see the perfect blue sky in the chilled quiet morning of the sports day (Undoukai) in late autumn.

"Painting to see the skies":
Drill two holes into a canvas.
Hang it where you can see the sky.
by Yoko Ono in 1961

I feel that I can share the same sensibility coming from the same origin in the East with her even though I have never met her and I will not be an icon of popular culture like her.

MACHIKO KONDO
Songs of Relief. Charcoal, conté, pastel on paper, 42" x 30"

40

MACHIKO KONDO

Songs of Amusement. Acrylic, charcoal, ink, pastel, linocut on paper, 42" x 30"

41

ANNA X.L. WONG
DEDICATION

Jade Snow Wong, writer, ceramicist

I was in junior high school when I first read *Fifth Chinese Daughter* by Jade Snow Wong. To this day, it is one of my most cherished books. Growing up in San Francisco Chinatown, I saw myself in her story. Jade Snow Wong's untiring pursuit of her dreams, her independence and her optimistic determination to succeed against many hardships showed a tenacious confidence. Her strength to keep her family traditions and values while at the same time, learning to fit into the American culture, gave me newfound hope, inspiration and courage to work hard for what I believe in.

ANNA X.L. WONG
Silence. Mixed media, 14" x 7"

ANNA X.L. WONG

Journey: East to West. Mixed media, 10" x 7"

KATHERINE AOKI
DEDICATION

Lynda Barry, cartoonist

Lynda Barry is a well-known cartoonist of Filipino ancestry. She is the author of Ernie Pook's *Comeek*, which I read when I was in college. I'm drawn to her direct delivery of sticky emotional issues. I also enjoy her distinct drawing style. Her work encourages me to create and say what I must in my own way.

KATHERINE AOKI
Right on Schedule. Linoleum cut with watercolor, 14" x 15"

RISHA WONG
DEDICATION

Genny Lim, Nellie Wong, Maxine Hong Kingston, Connie Young Yu, Bharati Mukherjee and Meena Alexander, writers

Asian American artists who have inspired me the most have been the poets Genny Lim, Nellie Wong and authors Maxine Hong Kingston, Connie Young Yu, Bharati Mukherjee and Meena Alexander. I have been reading all of their works for many years. In the 80s I read one of Genny's poems in a women's studies class in Oregon. I think it was called, "Wonder Women." My poems started getting published in the 90s. I have become friends with Nellie, Connie and Genny and they are wonderful people. Connie's writings on Californian APAs have helped shape my own writing style, as have the works of Bharati and Meena. In 1999, I did research work on South Asian women writers in India. Maxine's fiction has greatly influenced my short stories. One of my favorite books by her is *Tripmaster Monkey*. Nellie's sister, Flo, is an artist and her rice sack artworks are wonderful.

KALI YUGA
RISHA WONG

a wanted poster / in a post office / someone graffitis 'white trash' / over your haole face

your kkk letter / laughs at African aborigines, the Holocaust, Asians / it calls the Dalai Lama / the anti-Christ

your greenbacks detonate / regurgitate greed / poisons a sacred union / confederate flags on the victory mount / love lost for aeons

the kali yuga winds down / spirits rip / hungry ghosts return / in a nuclear age

emptiness is all / change—the only constant

six generations in America / perpetual foreigners / treading water in a sea / of ignorance

elitism and / privilege reign / nonaction is action / a silence that deafens / sounds of a hollow home / piercing

cries for justice / invisibility / true friends gather

a blind man rattles / his metal cup for coins / no legs / kind faced yogi / dispossessed / serenely unshaken by life

Zen nuns tell us to / kill the Buddha / if we meet him / kill the ego

SHARI ARAI DEBOER
DEDICATION

Mine Okubo, artist

While held in internment camps during World War II, Mine Okubo recorded daily life in her drawings. When I read her book, *Citizen 13660*, many years ago, I valued her observations of simple daily activities. The images gave me a better understanding of life as an internee and as my parents experienced it. In later years, Okubo followed her own artistic path staying true to her own voice, not an easy thing to do and a quality I strive for in my own life.

SHARI ARAI DEBOER
In the Shade. Intaglio print, 16" x 6"

SHARI ARAI DeBOER

Transient Rooms. Intaglio print, 12" x 9"

SUZANNE KIMIKO ONODERA

Untitled (Green). Oil on canvas, 50" x 38"

Suzanne Kimiko Onodera
Dedication

Florence Yoo, singer/songwriter, musician, actress, comedian

I remember the first day I met Florence Yoo. We were both attending the California College of the Arts and we just happened to sit next to each other in a Women's Art History class. She introduced herself to me and began a very long detailed story about her mother in Chicago. The story was sarcastic, bizarre and had a piercing wit. It was the beginning of a friendship that has lasted many years and across all of the states in the union she has called her home. Florence currently lives in Brooklyn, NY, and is fearlessly pursuing her career as a singer/songwriter, musician, actress and comedian. Florence's unique brand of comedy and song writing squeezes to the surface all of the uncomfortable questions about life, race, sexuality and tradition. I credit her for teaching me to work hard on my craft, to keep pushing even when the rejection letters just keep coming and to maintain a solid focus during the hard times. Most of all, it is her humor that sticks with me and continues to fuel the need to create, to take risks and to live life with passion. And her music is pretty darn good too.

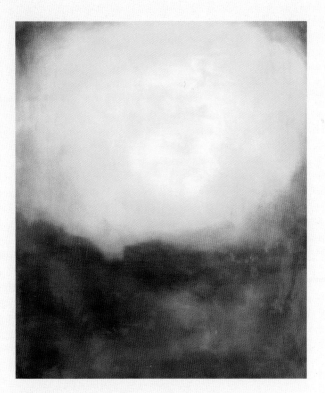

Suzanne Kimiko Onodera
In the Carmine Dream II. Oil on canvas, 60" x 48"

CATHERINE
CENIZA CHOY
DEDICATION

Helen Toribio, professor, activist

The narratives we construct and impart in academic teaching and research do matter in the "real world." They are integral to the continued success of social justice movements. Author, activist, teacher and mentor Helen Toribio, who passed away in the fall of 2004, exemplified these truths throughout her life. And she continues to do so in her legacy. I feel privileged to have received a little bit of Helen's mentorship. I will always admire her scholarship and her commitment to Filipino American students and studies more broadly. Throughout her life, Helen encouraged students to bridge their education with social justice issues. The new Helen Toribio Legacy Fund donates an internship grant to enable an organization to hire a young adult to work on progressive community issues.

HOW TO STAND UP AND DIVE
CATHERINE CENIZA CHOY

My six-year-old daughter Maya bobs up and down in the pool water smiling all the while. Her slender body makes the water gurgle and ripple just so. Thick strands of sopping wet hair stick to her face, partly covering an eye here, curling along the roundness of her nose there. She does not seem to mind. I enjoy watching her like this as if I can feel her joy of being in the water. Tired clichés of parenthood fill my mind. Yes, nothing can prepare you for being a parent. They indeed grow up so fast. Yes, learn to understand the power of now. While these statements hold truths, I find myself continually reflecting on the past in the present. As I smile and wave at her from the bleachers, I remember the way she made ripples in my womb. How her kicks made small half spheres that popped up from my then pregnant belly. Now her body makes waves in the water of Martin Luther King Pool, a public pool run by the city of Berkeley. How ironic, I chuckle uncomfortably to myself recalling a moment in February, Black History month.

I am standing next to Maya, who is perched on a step stool so that she can watch herself brush her teeth in the bathroom mirror. She swishes water in her mouth and spits it out, leaving a trace of toothpaste foam on her lips. "Mommy, are we black or white?" Although I am physically and mentally exhausted, thoughts unfurl quickly. I have spent much of my career challenging the dual nature of U.S. race relations. I live in the Bay Area where the significant presence of Asian Americans complicates this binary. I teach on a campus where Asian Americans comprise the largest group of people of color. And yet here stands my daughter, toothpaste foam dribbling down her chin, thinking of the world around her in terms of black and white. The academic language I have become accustomed to—racialization, Orientalism, panethnicity—does not translate well in this situation. I tell her, "We are neither. I am a second generation Filipino American. Daddy is a third generation Korean and Chinese American. You are a third generation Filipino American and a fourth generation Korean and Chinese American." I know my response does not have the catchiness of "black" or "white" and sure enough Maya responds, "But Martin Luther King said we were black or white." Later when Maya is in her pajamas and lying in bed, I tell her that Martin Luther King believed in the equality of people of all colors. He stood up for the belief that we are and can be many things. I tell her that she is a talented artist, an amazing reader, an impressive dancer, and now a budding swimmer. I look into her eyes and whisper these truths: "You are a wonderful big sister. You are my most perfect daughter." I say to her as well as to myself this plea: "Please do not forget this."

Maya is in a level one-plus swimming class. She is learning how to float on her belly and her back using what her instructors refer to as "starfish" moves, arms and legs spread out from her sides. "Watch me do the starfish, Mama," Maya would later say during a family swim day, proudly demonstrating her new swimming maneuvers. At the conclusion of the two-week intensive course, she will receive a progress sheet that lists seventeen skills needed to pass level one-plus. None of the skills refer to starfish. Skill number three is the "back float with recovery (unsupported)" and skill number four is "front float with recovery (unsupported)."

The word "dive" also does not appear on the list of skills. But on one of the final days, the instructors tell the children to climb out of the shallow part of the pool and line up at its edge. They must take turns jumping feet first into the pool. When it is Maya's turn, I see some hesitation in her body. Instead of jumping up and over the edge, her body tenses, she crouches down and jumps in (well, scoots in, would probably be more accurate) barely making a splash. I do not think much of her hesitation until the following day when she and her classmates are instructed to climb out of the shallow end of the pool and walk over in a line to the deeper end. With two instructors in the water, they are supposed to take turns jumping in. I find myself nervous for Maya. I read fear in the way her body stiffens, the way her eyes cast downward. No joy here.

It is Maya's turn to plunge in the deep water. The instructors' voices are muffled, but I hear sounds of encouragement. Maya's toes curl against the rim of the pool's edge. She heeds the instructors' words, but fear jolts her shoulders back each time she leans forward preparing for her jump. I hear other parents coo as they watch her. "She's so small. She's so cute." But my body tenses too. When she first jumps in, her body is so stiff, that she lands almost face flat into the water making a huge splash, the water slapping against her hard. And yet Maya pulls her body up out of the water only to jump back in. Again and again. Her body continues to hesitate with each time. But she continues to stand up and dive.

A blowing whistle signals the end of class. I rush over to her and drape a towel over her shoulders. I tell her with the biggest smile I can muster, "I am so proud of you. You were terrific." I say this over and over as her body shivers and shakes from the coolness of the air as well as her struggle to fight back the tears. For the time being, she is not proud. She does not feel terrific. Later, she receives her progress report stating matter of factly that she has passed level one-plus and can move on to level two.

I know when something is wrong even though Maya laughs, tells stories and plays games like nothing is wrong. I go along with the typically playful behavior until her eyebrows crinkle and tears well up and I know we will have to confront what's bothering her. And this time it is not difficult for me to predict that Maya is unhappy about moving on to level two. Because in level two you begin to learn strokes that move you from one end of the shallow pool to the other. You are almost in constant motion. You do not play water games like "Mr. Fox" and "Marco Polo." And with these certainties, comes uncertainty. How will you do in level two, where some of the kids are "big" kids who are in second and maybe even third grade? The tears stream down her cheeks and some mucous bubbles at the tip of her nose. "Please," she pleads, "I don't want to be in level two." She continues while choking back her tears, so that her voice sounds like gasps of air, "I don't want to go swimming anymore." "Not swim anymore?" I respond in disbelief. "You are so talented in the water," I tell her. "You look so natural as you bob and float and kick." I realize that I am raising my voice at her. And that does not help matters.

We do not continue to speak about this while Maya

*Constance Chang aka Chang Shangpu,
artist*

I dedicate my painting to Chang Shangpu, known in the Bay Area as Constance Chang. Our painting styles are nothing alike, and I am a callow amateur to her long distinguished career as an artist. It is the intersection of identities and experiences in her work that speaks to me: She is a Chinese immigrant to the United States, a war survivor, a woman-artist in a male-dominated art world. I am a bi-racial woman struggling to find my voice, whether in my own heart or in its resonance in the world around me. We both choose art as the instrument of expression. I will never forget walking into the Asian Art Museum of San Francisco and hearing so clearly her inimitable voice singing through the paintings splashed along the walls. Since that day, I am continually inspired by her ability to push classical Chinese calligraphy and ink work towards modernist abstraction, at the same time defying any one style. I will always admire not only the unique path in painting she has forged, but also its reflection of a life of beauty, discipline, wisdom, expression and insight.

brushes her teeth and changes into her pajamas. But when she lies down on her bed, I tell her that swimming is much more than a level one or level two class. "First," I explain, "it's great exercise for the body." "You mean, swimming is a sport?!" Maya asks incredulously. I nod my head. I tell her how I did not learn how to swim until I was in college at the very relatively old age of twenty. By that time, I had had the opportunity to visit some amazing parts of the world: Belize in Central America and Kenya in East Africa. During both those journeys, my inability to swim impacted what I could experience. In Belize, I jumped off a boat with a friend thinking I would be able to tread or float in the water. But upon breaking the surface of the water, panic spread over me and I spent the rest of the afternoon desperately climbing back into the boat and nursing the bruises forming along the backs of arms. At the coast of Kenya, I was hanging out with two friends on a beach when they decided to explore an empty boat anchored close to the shore. The water was calm, but I told them to go ahead and they swam on without me. "So second," I continue, "swimming is more than something that's good for you. It can enrich your life. When I finally learned to swim a lap in college, when I was twenty years old, mind you, I can still remember how good it felt, how good I felt when my hand touched the pool's edge. I had done something I was unable to do before, something I thought many times before I would never be able to do."

Maya is having trouble falling asleep from the stress of the impending level two class. So I reach for one more story to tell. "Once upon a time," I begin, "there was a girl who was born in San Francisco. Her name was Victoria Manalo. Victoria's daddy was from the Philippines. Her mommy was from England. Victoria did not learn to swim until she was about nine or ten. She was much, much older than you. Can you imagine? She was afraid of the water, which meant that she missed out on playing games in the water like 'Mr. Fox.' Can you imagine that? But when Victoria was much, much older, when she was a teenager, she was interested in learning how to dive. But in the 1920s and 1930s, people in California were not kind to Filipinos even though Filipinos did very difficult farm labor that other people did not want to do. A swimming and diving coach in San Francisco separated Victoria from the other swimmers and divers because she was part Filipino. And then he insisted that Victoria use her mother's English last name, Taylor, instead of her father's Filipino last name, Manalo. Victoria faced many challenges. But she faced her fears about being in the water and learned to love to dive in it. She faced people who did not like her because she was Filipino, but she continued to love herself and treasure both her Daddy's and Mommy's backgrounds. And, can you imagine, Victoria Manalo went on to win two gold medals in diving at the Olympic Games, a competition that includes swimmers and divers from all over the world. All over the world! In 1948, Victoria became the first woman ever in Olympic history to win two gold medals in two individual diving events. It's good to know who Martin Luther King was and what he stood for. It's also important to know who Victoria Manalo is and what she accomplished. Do not be afraid, little one. Just enjoy being in the water, moving across it, smiling as you bob in it."

The next morning as we walk over to the pool, I doubt that anything I said the previous night mattered. Maya whimpered and whined through breakfast and during our walk she does little different. When we arrive at that part of the pool where we must separate—I must go to the bleachers and she to the shallow pool's edge, I think about saying, "Remember the story I told you about Victoria," but I do not. I know that these stories do indeed matter, but I think that they must be told again and again in order for the worlds of the listeners to re-shape, bend, look different. I tell myself, it takes time for these narratives to seep into the bones of our being. But then, as I watch Maya enter the pool, I think that perhaps it may not take as long as one might think. "Stand up and jump in," her instructor calls out to her. So Maya stands straight and plunges in, feet first, body straight. No hesitation. No fear. From the bleachers I can see that she is looking up at her instructor waiting for what comes next. And she is smiling.

SUMMER MEI LING LEE
Grandmother. Oil, 4' x 4'

LYDIA NAKASHIMA DEGARROD

Unjust Death. Mixed media, 30" x 32"

Lydia Nakashima Degarrod

Dedication

Maxine Hong Kingston, writer

I am dedicating these paintings to Maxine Hong Kingston, a Chinese American writer, for creating an Asian heroine who validated many of my childhood fantasies of defending the powerless. While reading *The Woman Warrior* as a young student in Hawaii, I encountered for the first time an Asian heroine who rebelled against the tyrants and defended the weak. I had grown up in a tiny community of people of Japanese descent in Chile, where I had little access to Japanese culture. My contact with the culture of half of my ancestors came primarily from the Japanese Samurai films I watched at the embassy. It was while watching these Samurai films that I fantasized about saving the weak. With her magic of writing, Hong Kingston allowed me to relive those childhood dreams, and to realize that the power of the imagination and art can give courage to express any form of injustice and empower the dispossessed.

Lydia Nakashima Degarrod
Urban Seekers II. Mixed media, 30" x 22"

ZILKA JOSEPH
DEDICATION

Chitra Bannerjee Divakaruni, writer

My first friend in the U.S., Joe, an admirer of Chitra Bannerjee Divakaruni, gave me *Arranged Marriage* just weeks after I arrived from Calcutta. I was homesick and lonely, and the women in her stories cried out to me. I had to stop reading. I took some time to pick it up again. Joe gave me more of her books, all signed. Her poem collections *Black Candle* and *The Unknown Errors of our Lives* spoke to me once more. Among the voices there, I heard my own, felt that uncanny resonance. Some years later, I began to write again. I explored my memories, my life, shared my story. Ms. Divakaruni's work helped me validate my experience, write what I know, and I learned to celebrate myself. Thank you, Ms. Divakaruni. Thank you, Joe.

HERA LEE
DEDICATION

Maxine Hong Kingston, writer; Maya Lin, architect; Michelle Wie, golfer

I find great strength from three contemporary Asian American women. Maxine Hong Kingston, writer, whose peaceful resolve to speak her voice far outreaches her diminutive form; Maya Lin, whose artistic force is free of self-consciousness, and serves as an inspiration to all artists; Michelle Wie, whose youth, physical stature and confident moxie are a wonderful harbinger of the future of Asian American women.

GREEN CARD
ZILKA JOSEPH

On a blazing summer day, we are last in line

standing at the end of a long vinyl shelter

swelling like a hot air balloon

full of stale perfume, restless feet,

b.o. and icy palms, just

at that very edge where

the rays of sun reach in and grab our ankles.

Listening to many languages,

guessing what they say,·

shifting from foot to foot,

we crawl closer to the door.

It is nearly two hours,

we can go inside now.

The air conditioning cools

the beads at our temples.

We are frisked,

then line up again,

against the wall.

Children with bubble-gum

stuck to their sandals

scramble onto laps or try to climb walls.

We sit in hard chairs

waiting for our number to be called.

Faces, tired, tense,

from every nation wait too.

An old man with no teeth

and green sweat pants is helped inside

by a young man wearing Harley Davidson boots.

They speak little English,

t-shirts shriek Tommy Hilfiger, Florida,

Six Flags America.

Those desperate to suck cigarettes,

rush outside, come back in quickly—

Green cards dangle in the balance.

The sharp edge of my blue passport

rips the envelope,

nudges my hand. It remembers

the old country,

dust still sits in its creases,

knows its days are numbered,

and like a cat in a cage,

mute with fright

all eyes,

lets itself be taken to

undisclosed destinations.

MIJIN LEE
DEDICATION

Lois-Ann Yamanaka, writer

The first Asian American writer I encountered was Lois-Ann Yamanaka in my Asian American Literature class at college. I was struck by *Wild Meat* and *The Bully Burgers,* which I stumbled upon at the library postgrad; her writing was incredibly raw and unapologetic and her characters quirky and endearing. It's the type of writing I admire because of its fierce honesty and fearlessness of being yourself no matter the raised eyebrows. I need that in my life—to not apologize for who I am.

ARRIVALS AND DEPARTURES

MIJIN LEE

The first man I fell in love with didn't know how to kiss me. But he knew how to Eskimo kiss—pressing his nose against mine, his pupils like steady rain. He knew how to rest his face in the crook of my neck, his breath a silk scarf. He didn't know how to hold my hand; it would slip out of his as if my hand had turned to water. I let him hold my laughter, but he let that slip through his fingers as well. He didn't know what to do with it. His packaged laughter was like lace—its webs tickling my palms like a spider's many legs. I had always wondered what his unleashed laughter would feel like in my hands. I imagined it to be like a horse's hooves nearly crushing my bones.

The second man I fell in love with sketched lost things on my arm and back with his curved finger as if he were drawing in sand. I wanted to find them for him and tried to memorize the pictures before the sands sifted. I looked at the palm of his right hand and traced the lines with my finger. His map was unclear and I became lost, trying to understand why I couldn't rescue him. Once, I found his kiss that tasted of raspberries and purred like velvet. It was quick like a hummingbird, ending before I knew it had started.

The third man I fell in love with could not look me in the eyes. I forgot who I was and drifted into separate continents, divided and silenced. His tongue was a thorn, his hands cold like metal. My lips traveled the rises and falls of his face to make sure it was him. He showed me his storms and earthquakes that trembled and throbbed. But he wouldn't let me step into them—afraid the winds would knock me down and the broken earth swallow me. They found me anyway. And so I watched him shrink among the disasters that swelled as the wind would slap my eyes and possess my hair to dance like demons. Everyone else was held off with an empty smile, unable to see the burdens he carried, fooled like I'd been before. In the spring when the snow had melted, I cut him from my life and cut my hair so that it ceased to dance as if possessed.

The fourth man I fell in love with played a song on my arm with his fingers that longed and found, then longed again. I thought the song would resonate forever. His music was familiar like sunlight and warm tea; it seeped in to become a part of me like the salt on my lips, the oil in my hair and the curve of my hips. When I kissed his widow's peak and the lobes of his ears there was weeping in his sigh. Distance blurred the time we had together and confused me as to which world was real. His words filled certain spaces in my soul and my words did the same for him. We parted when it was time and took those words with us as armor and shield.

The fifth man I was beginning to fall in love with kissed my right shoulder as if it were his child. His touch was rain my skin drank in and then smelled of dew. When we kissed hard, he pulled me into his chest, our bodies pressed like hands clasped in prayer. We both wanted because we wouldn't have the time to know enough. We had slipped off caution and practicality, stretching into desire to give and receive. His face became soft and easy to love as the second hand ticked towards sunrise, my shuttle, the airport, and departing plane. It ticked away from the petals that cooled us, from the fire that licked and reminded me of how to burn. I reached to touch the scarlet morning sky and raindrops from the night, trembling on his windshield like stars.

The sixth man I fell in love with rose tall like a tree and still with life. Our fingers entwined, vines braided and covered with spring's first green. My cheek rested against his chest to hear his heart beat beneath the fabric of his coat, and his fingers brushed like eyelashes against my other cheek. He spoke my mother's tongue; his words and silence that listened—a womb that enclosed me. His veins blushed hot and his hand rested on my collarbone or spread across my belly, branding my flesh. This was our language we both understood. He leaned over, his hair swaying and smelling of sun. He put his ear to my lips to hear me breathe and sigh. He crowned me with attention, insisting I wear his heart, though he knew I wouldn't stay.

The final man I fall in love with will hold a woman who knows how to Eskimo kiss. She will hold his laughter as if holding innocence. She will look at the palm of his hand and then watch him point out to her where he is. She will stay in one piece, because he will help to remind her who she is. She will sing songs for him while strumming his hair. She will listen to his heartbeat and he will let her listen. His hand will rest against the wall of her chest as he hums a tune to the rhythm of her heart. They will never know enough and become dizzy with beginnings. Their souls will twist into a braid so tight it can never be undone. This woman rides the bus with her nose pressed against the glass, in love with herself and all her ghosts and insecurities. A halo of steam leaks from her mouth; it spreads like life upon the glass that frames a moving city.

ELA SHAH
DEDICATION

Mira Nair, film director

My first memorable encounter with Mira
Nair, the acclaimed film director, was watching the movie *Mississippi Masala*. I was surprised and impressed by her frank discussion
of racial issues in an open and honest man-
ner. Her cinematography and direction was
also memorable. Mira Nair's work is both
entertaining and serious, motivated by multi-
culturalism and her interest in intense human
relationships, two topics I also express in my
work visually. Although I had never picked
up a hammer in my life, I was encouraged to
see that a woman of India could create such
good work in a male-oriented field. She inspired me to attempt to create massive sculptures and work with heavy machines, mascu-
line tasks I did not think I could accomplish.
Her work is also fundamentally Indian and
multiethnic simultaneously: her narratives
bridge gaps between cultures and transplant
stories that are unknown and magical to the
American psyche. She depicts worlds that
are both authentically Indian and universally
human. I want to tell such stories visually,
and create paintings and sculptures that are
rooted in India but transcend all cultures and
point towards universal truths.

ELA SHAH

Watch out America. Silver leaf, paint on burnt wood
and mixed media, 40" x 18" x 1"

Sharon Leong
Dedication

Anna May Wong, actress

About a year ago, I came across a biography of America's first notable Asian American actress, Anna May Wong. Anna grew up in Hollywood during the silent film era. Bitten by the acting bug, she had the courage and determination to follow her dream of becoming an accomplished actress, which not only went against the grain of her family's traditional Chinese mores, but her struggles to succeed were made even more daunting by what was then a racist and sexist film industry. Despite the stereotypical roles she was assigned, from playing Asian prostitutes to chambermaids, Anna nevertheless strove to hone her craft, eventually winning the hearts of audiences throughout the world. Nowadays Anna May Wong would be viewed as a liberated woman who, against familial, societal and professional pressures, followed her own heart. This was evidenced not only by her career choices as an actress, but also by her private life in which she broke taboos by having love affairs with married men. Anna's stance resonates deeply with me, as my lifelong struggle as an artist is to freely paint, and live, that which best represents me as an evolving individual, without kowtowing to cultural or societal norms. I draw inspiration from Anna's life, and celebrate it by dedicating this to her.

SHARON LEONG
Mothra. Acrylics, 20" x 16"

MELBA ABELA
DEDICATION

Loida Nicolas-Lewis, CEO, writer, political activist

I have never met Loida Nicolas-Lewis, yet I have known of her for decades, back when she was a student leader in law school and I was an undergraduate at the University of the Philippines. Even then she was already outstanding: highly intelligent, articulate and determined. These attributes continue to serve her well. As an immigrant lawyer educated in the Philippines, Nicolas-Lewis early on positioned herself as an able player in NYC's mostly white, male-dominated legal, business and financial communities. Among her major accomplishments are becoming the CEO of TLC Beatrice LLC, an author of best selling books and a political activist on behalf of disenfranchised minorities, including Filipino WWII veterans. Nicolas-Lewis exemplifies in the best sense all these concerns, having successfully crossed and re-crossed many borders and boundaries.

MELBA ABELA

This image and facing page: *Mudra IV: From the Halad Series*

Two views of interactive installation, Baybay Beach, Capiz, Philippines. Found shells, 10' x 8'

Photo courtesy of Togonon Gallery.

MELBA ABELA

This image and facing page: *Mudra IV: From the Halad Series*

Two views of interactive installation, Baybay Beach, Capiz, Philippines. Found shells, 10' x 8'

SHIZUE SEIGEL
DEDICATION

*Rui Sasaki and Nellie Nakamura, pioneers
and mothers*

In the year before she turned one hundred, I had the privilege to sit with Nellie Nakamura and listen to the stories of her family's women. Through Nellie, I learned that her mother Rui had been born in 1868, at the dawn of Japan's modern age, that she had run away from her arranged marriage and abandoned her samurai husband and infant son to travel the world with a Massachusetts spinster. Nellie is an "ordinary" woman who has nurtured and inspired Emmy the artist and Lisa the scholar, with their feet planted firmly on the ground, their heads full of stars, and eyes fixed on freedom.

DON'T LOOK AWAY

SHIZUE SEIGEL

Number 4 Sutter bus. San Francisco, 1960. The old man heads straight for the empty seat next to me and sits down. His scalp shows pink and freckled through thinning hair and the loose skin around his mouth is stubbled with silver. His chambray shirt and khakis are fairly clean, but he emits a powerful odor of sharp Caucasian sweat.

"Wawa ish ma rarr wa arr. Ararrr?" The tenor of his voice is calmly conversational, as if he were talking about the weather or youthful reminiscences. "Woh ma arr arrrrr," the man continues. He stares with fatherly intensity. *Don't make the same mistakes I made, kid,* says the tone, but the sounds are no known language. Polite little Asian American kid that I am, I try to look understanding and respectful, but I feel helpless, *I'm only a kid, why me?* "Arr wa rar rar," the old man says. His eyes translate: *You're a good kid. You'll be all right.*

The old man leaves his smell on the seat when he shuffles slowly down the aisle and off the bus. I steal a look at the other passengers. They're looking away, as if avoiding a deformity, intently not looking at where the old man had sat. I flush red, feeling guilt by association. Why me? I find myself eternally feeling like I don't quite measure up, my socks falling down, the hem of my skirt turned up, my slip showing. Why is it always me that the drunks and crazies sit next to? Do I have invisible cooties sticking to me, saying "weirdos welcome"?

Sixth Street Needle Exchange, San Francisco, October 1995. Tanya, a faithful regular at the Wednesday night exchange, always has kind words for the volunteers handing out alcohol swabs, syringes and sterilizing bleach. "How are you ladies doing tonight? That's good. So glad you're here. It's a great thing you're doing. You don't get paid do this, but you show up every week, making sure us junkies stay safe. Gotta be grateful for that."

Blunt-nosed, with broad Slavic cheekbones, Sonia's dressed for the street, with a heavy fake sheepskin carcoat and a knit cap jammed over blonde curls. She carries a big plastic milk crate slung over her shoulder. It's multi-purpose: a bag lady's tote crate, a begging stool, a step ladder and—arcing fast at the end of its long red strap—a dandy little shinbreaker. Tanya is ready for anything. She may be a junkie panhandler, but she moves through life as deliberately as a Safeway truck on a downtown street, unstoppably competent. The needles she turns in are always neatly bundled in groups of five, with nail polish marking "hers" from "his." "His" belong to Bill, her faithful shadow.

He doesn't come in but lingers watchfully outside while she ducks in to make the trade.

December 1995. Tanya drags in a new client. She's a bluff mother hen steering her little starveling by the elbow. The new client is a slight black man about 55, looking ready to cut and run, eyes flicking around the room. "Here you go," she coos. "You drop the points into the bucket here, but you gotta do it slow, so the lady can count. It's a one-for-one exchange. They can't give you no extras."

Tanya talks constantly, telling us volunteers what she did, what she's going to do, what her landlord told her and how much cat litter costs at the corner store. Since she noticed the chronic fungus condition that stiffens my right index finger, she makes a point of asking about it every week. "How's the finger doing? Let me see." She takes my hand gently and examines the coarsened skin. Smiling reassuringly, she always says, "That's looking better!" even when it's clearly not.

An hour later, as I wait for the bus at a Tenderloin streetcorner, I see Tanya as she veers away from Bill with a shout. "Fuck it! Just fuck it." She stumbles blindly down the street, tear-glazed eyes not recognizing my face or hearing my hello. Bill's placatory gesture dies half-made. He hitches his shoulders with practiced patience and trails after Tanya, twenty paces behind, waiting for her to calm down. He doesn't notice me either.

Montgomery Street, November 1996. Tanya stands in the street at the edge of late-afternoon traffic, her hand stretched out, beseeching the Audis, Miatas and BMWs that rush past in a blind metallic stream. Eyes blank, she bites her lip. Her face is taut with unshed tears.

"Tanya!" I say. "How's it going?" Her eyes widen in recognition and relief. She seizes me with the desperation of someone publicly drowning in a torrent of indifference.

"Hi! It's you! So good to see you!" She tries for her customary heartiness, but her voice cracks. "It's not going so great. Not so great today." Her eyes well up, and in an instant, she's a blubbery mess, tears and snot streaming. "We've been out here all day and we've made two dollars and eleven cents. We haven't eaten all day.... I try, you know...I really try. But sometimes it's so hard." I put my arm around her and pull her out of the street and onto the sidewalk. The pedestrians divide around us like a river around a couple of rocks.

"Where's Bill?"

"Oh, he's over there." Tanya waves toward Bill, who is standing across the street, next to Sonia's all-purpose milk crate. He's not quite looking at us, but his body leans toward us, rigid with concern.

"It'll be okay, Tanya. You're tripping 'cause you're hungry." I hand her five bucks which I can't really afford. "You'll feel better if you have something to eat."

Tanya sniffles. "You're so good, I..."

I cut her off. Looking her straight in the eye, I speak slowly and emphatically. "Tanya, you're good. I know how good you are. And God knows. Don't let the assholes get you down."

"Yeah...I just need to eat," she tells herself. "Yeah," she says, her voice firmer. "Okay. OKAY!" She pats her pockets for a kleenex. She straightens her shoulders and her voice brightens. "It's so good to see you. How've you been? How's your finger. Oh look, there's Bill. He must be worried." She heads towards him. As she crosses the street, she looks back over her shoulder. "Take care, baby," she calls to me. "See you Wednesday."

After that, every time she sees me at the needle exchange, Tanya greets me like a life-long friend. Mostly. Sometimes she is too distraught or too intent on copping to notice me.

Sixth Street Needle Exchange. December 1996. One Wednesday a few weeks later, as we leave the exchange, Tanya asks, "Say, have I ever shown you a picture of my daughter?"

"I didn't know you had one."

"Yeah. Oh yeah!" She rolls her eyes with delight. She digs through her pockets and fishes out a photo of a plump and pretty teenager. "Melody. She's fifteen. Isn't she pretty? And smart as a whip." She pulls out a thick, dog-eared stack of Polaroids held together by a rubber band. She shows me pictures of Melody as a toddler, as a little girl, with her dog, with her grandmother, in front of a car. Tanya rattles off a running commentary full of minute details and big gaps. I piece together a ragged story of small-town roots and early ruin. Tanya's born-again mother had been stiff-necked and disapproving of blowsy blonde Tanya, puppy-fat and buxom and pregnant too soon. The wrong men and drink and drugs and Melody growing up with grandma in the podunk valley town.

"I haven't seen her in fifteen months. My mother thinks I'm a bad influence." She laughs dryly. "And I guess I am…. But I'm going to clean up. I'm going to get my daughter back. Bill and I could get a bigger place. She could stay with us. I just need to get my act together…." The sentence trails off as if she doesn't believe herself.

"I miss her so much," she says after a pause. "Isn't she beautiful? And smart, too."

Over the next year, Tanya looks worse and worse, her skin gets patchy and breaks out in little sores. My heart clutches when I see her. I feel powerless to help her, or any of the other clients. All I can do is keep showing up and loving them for a couple of minutes apiece twice a month.

"I love your tattoo." I say to the gen-Xer whose slender neck is banded with delicate indigo antelopes. "Whatchya got on today? Girl, you got style!" to the black woman in the crushed velvet coat from Goodwill. "Love your kit. That's so cool!" to the raw-boned transgender who keeps her paraphernalia in a pink plastic Barbie lunchbox. Silently I pray for each of them, wondering what life has to offer them if they do clean up. They have so many challenges to deal with. Many are in poor health, have learning disabilities and lack job skills. They are black, gay, incest survivors, victims of family violence. *Only this moment. Only love*, I remind myself. It's all I can do.

November 1997. I'm crossing the street to the bus stop at Market and Montgomery, going home after yet another meeting on an HIV prevention project for low-income women. I have just learned that the money that has been promised for over a year will be redirected to the police department. I'm struggling with anger and disappointment when I see Tanya at the bus stop.

"Tanya!"

"Oh, hi!" Tanya greets me as if she'd just seen me yesterday, although in fact, it's been months since I've seen her or Bill at the needle exchange.

"I was wondering what happened to you. How have you been?"

"I'm great! Just great! I got into a program." I examine her face as she rattles on about the methadone program. The blotches and sores have cleared up and there's a new strength and firmness in her features.

"Tanya, you're looking great." Out of the corner of my eye, I see Bill hurrying towards the bus stop. When he sees me, he breaks out in a wide grin and raises his hand in delighted greeting. I'm swept up in the tide of Tanya's chatter, and slow to return the wave, so Bill's already looking away by the time I react. But that brief flash of unadulterated welcome is the first unguarded moment I've ever seen in him.

We all get on the same bus. I sit next to Bill, and Tanya sits opposite, still talking her drug rehabilitation program. "I'm trying to get Bill to go, but he had a bad experience with methadone." Bill starts to say something, but Tanya overrides him. "He was on methadone once before, see, and he got busted, so he had to go cold turkey in jail. See, he's got a temper, you know.... But not lately. This was six, seven years ago...." I nod. I have heard that kicking methadone cold is even more unpleasant than kicking heroin. I turn to Bill as Tanya keeps talking.

Feeling my eyes on him, he asks about my finger. "How long's it been messed up? Four years?" he shakes his head.

"I been praying on that finger."

"Tanya's been doing great," he continues. "And she's doing it for herself. Not for her daughter, not for me. For her own self. I'm so proud of her. I knew she could do it."

"And how about you, Bill?" He's been looking past me with the practiced self-effacement of a small man trying to stay out of trouble on the street. "I been knowing you for two years now. You're quiet and you hang back, but I been watching you." Bill sneaks a look at me. I grin back. "I seen how smart you are and how you look after Tanya. You guys are a great team."

Bill nods. His eyes sheen with unshed tears. He's used to not being noticed.

"You can kick it, too. If not with methadone, maybe some other program. I feel you, Bill. You're a good man. You may be quiet, but down deep, you're strong, and you got a real good heart."

As I talk, Bill seems to expand, straightening his shoulders and breathing a little deeper with the quiet dignity of a middle-aged man with nothing more to prove. He's looking at me full-on now, his warm brown eyes taking in every word. I lean gently into his shoulder. "I know you can do it. I'll be praying for you."

"Thank you," he says softly, with resolve.

"Here's our stop," Tanya says. "Do you still go to the women's needle exchange in the Mission? Make sure they have flyers up for the drug program. They still got slots open for the next session. You should put up some flyers." Tanya continues to talk as she and Bill pull the cord for their stop, walk down the aisle and step off the bus. "Take care of that finger, now. Good to see you."

In the sudden silence after the door closes behind them, I realize that we'd all been talking pretty loud. I glance down the aisle and see that other passengers are staring straight ahead, looking away as if from a deformity.

NORINE NISHIMURA
DEDICATION

Sachiko Yvonne Nakamura, performing artist

Sachiko Yvonne Nakamura, born a Scorpio in 1941, died a diva in 2004. She was a performance artist, an improvisational master, a community mainstay and my first vivid introduction to myself. She had moved in as a replacement roommate when I was 19, impacting my life first as an intimate confidante, which expanded to artistic and romantic director, urging me to live my art as fully as I lived my life. She wrote and directed perhaps the first all–Asian American performance piece as her masters thesis in the early 70s and co-founded the Asian American Dance Collective in San Francisco. Moving forward to more eclectic spheres of creative genius, Sachi continued working through her life issues both on and off stage. It was on her last morning that she gave me her most profound teaching, that our connection with all life is, in fact, infinite, immeasurable and immutably rooted in love.

NORINE NISHIMURA
Sterile Cuckoo. Acrylics, pencil, 40.5" x 26"

Monsters

Nancy Hom

It is easy to blame old monsters that reside in caves in my mind.

How else to explain the sudden scream of words hurled at my daughter tonight?

Once unleashed, they could not be contained.

I let them have their feast by her throat.

I recall my mother, who sewed regrets into pajamas

and wore them inside out. She rolled her sleeves

so I could see how the rough fabric had pricked her skin

and left it raw where a dream should have been.

And my father, in white shirts even on Chinese New Year,

serving cocktails and wontons till four in the morning seven days a week.

At night I waited for the turn of the police lock

and heard the creak of the mattress as he sighed his way into bed.

Instead of dreams they gave me words, which I saved like chicken bones in a tin box.

The words grew into monsters that hissed in the dark.

They tore my dresses into shreds, scratched my guitar, broke my mirror in two.

They have stayed with me through the years, waiting for nights like this.

The next morning my daughter shuffles to the table, head down,

eyes puffed like melon balls. As my mother did before me,

I push a rice bowl toward her. Salivating, the monsters hover, but I beat them back.

"I'm sorry," I murmur, and she begins to eat.

THE HOUSE
MAW SHEIN WIN

1

she had a dream night after night from the age of 8. it lasted 2 years. it was the same dream again and again.

the setting could have been ireland or scotland. this is what her family thought when she would describe the landscape. the green land with low rolling green hills, dotted with trees. imbued with hope.

not like the landscape of rangoon. the strangle of trees and vines. the oppressive house on the edge of the lake.

2

there is a story she likes to tell; when my father was growing up. as the eldest and the brightest, my father would always sit at the head of the table, eating an entire chicken cooked to his liking, as his younger brother looked on. a small portion of rice on his plate.

3

los angeles. a looming two story converted into a monastery for sri lankan buddhist monks. it is my mother's ordination day. she will be a nun. my oldest sister is there. dressed inappropriately as usual in a tight short black dress with a removable sparkly tattoo on her arm. her new older boyfriend is with her. she is sobbing.

4

my mother looks through the windows facing the bay. sometimes i watch her. she doesn't know i'm there. she reminds me of our cat sitting on her perch in meditative thought. in the distance one can see the bridge. the cars barely visible in the early light.

5

aunty oh wears bright red lipstick when she wants to be happy. she owns many longyis and the one she wears today is cream colored with big aqua polka dots. gold bangles, a ruby around her smooth thanaka covered neck.

6

the house in apple valley. cactus depresses me. the landscape makes me
feel as if i were dropped off on the moon, alone, on the way to kmart in
our brown toyota wagon. my parents forget to pick me up.

7

the golden stupas peek out through the clutches of trees. the plane lands.

8

the dream goes like this.
she sees a house.
it is a mansion.
four huge white pillars.
she can see it.
she can see it clearly.
so real, she would tell baba.
so real.

9

freckles across the landscape of her cheekbones. a
constellation from a past life.
maybe she was born live in that house.

MELANI NAGAO
Haleko. Acrylics, 20" x 16"

OLIVIA BOLER
DEDICATION

Sigrid Nuñez, writer

In graduate school, my goals were to figure out my subject matter and to discover my "voice," the aspiring writer's holy grail. What I wanted to write about and the way I would write about it were somehow connected. The few pieces I had written as an adult were tentative, pale imitations of authors—women and men, mostly white from the East Coast or Europe or the 19th century—who had nothing in common with me, a San Francisco hapa girl. One of my professors recommended Sigrid Nuñez's *A Feather on the Breath of God*, a novel about an ordinary young woman who is half-Chinese and half-Caucasian—a woman like me. After reading this book, I realized with relief that writing from my dual yet divided perspective was unavoidable. How freeing! I'm forever grateful to Ms. Nuñez for helping me find my subject matter, and my voice.

ON THE WALL
OLIVIA BOLER

APPLICATION—PART THREE—ESSAY

In the space below, please tell us more about yourself and your reasons for applying to our program. Feel free to attach additional pages if needed.

The first time I remember turning into a fly, I still slept in a cradle and the whole thing was beyond my control. I recall my mother came into my room and sifted through my blankets. Her eyes hunted the furniture, but it was a small space, more of a walk-in closet, and the only other place a toddler could go was behind a very large teddy bear I just this second remember having. Anyway, my mother turned around, left the room, and came back in, scared and panicked. She glanced up and saw me hanging out in the corner of the ceiling. I'd been watching her the whole time, upside down and sideways. She stood there forever, just staring at me. Eventually she turned around and shut the door. And eventually, somehow, I must have turned back into a human baby without crashing to the floor or causing too much bodily harm. I mean, here I am.

The next time I was older, maybe going to preschool, and we were at the dinner table. She was trying to make me eat bitter melon and liver. Even coated in my mother's special hot pepper and soy sauce combo, I hated it. But instead of crying or holding my breath—pop!—I took wing.

"You don't get this from my side of the family," she said as I buzzed around her head. That's when she told me the truth about what had happened to my father. He had not been, as I had always been led to believe, killed in the line of duty, a policeman, one of SFPD's finest. No. He had been swatted to death by one of our neighbors one night after he and my mother fought over whether or not they should sell his 1973 Moto Guzzi. He'd left in a huff, zipped out the window straight into Mrs. Ip's flyswatter. Slam. Bam. Mother sold the motorcycle and put the money in the bank. My college fund. There are times I wonder if she set him up.

I have considered following in my father's footsteps, becoming a policeman or, to be politically correct as well as syntactically accurate, a police officer. I am a woman, as you know. A fly-woman. I've sometimes wondered why a fly. Why not something with a little more style, a little less association with dog crap and garbage? That's what I used to wish—not that I could be "normal," but that if I had to transform, I could at least be a thing of beauty—a butterfly or dragonfly or, heck, even a moth.

• • •

Naturally, you literary types—I presume there are a few of you in this "industry"—think, Kafka. How do you think *he* got the idea? Every fiction springs from truth.

I have only used my powers for good. *My* good. In grade school, I was the class pariah. It's like the other kids knew. I don't know how. We weren't poor. I was clean, had nice clothes, long hair my mother tied in ribbons—I had the same kind of clothes, ribbons, and hair like all the other girls. I wasn't a big baby—I didn't cart a blankie to school, not like some of the kids. I toted a regular lunchbox with some age-appropriate superhero on it—Wonder Woman or Goldie Gold. Still, my classmates detested me and reveled in their hatred. In the school yard, I got swatted on more than one occasion by the popular girls, the tough kids, even the nerds.

The third time I turned, I was eight, crying in a restroom. The popular girls had been ripping into my new Kangaroos shoes, which were an unfortunate poop color, but on sale, and every kid had to have them, the little zip pocket so choice for stashing a quarter or two. Nifty or not, my new tennies were ugly, and those girls let me know it. As if that weren't bad enough, one of them shoved me, and I fell into a bush, scratching my face on the branches. I ran into the building, not sure where to go, and finally settled on the bathroom for a good cry. A few minutes later, snot dripping over my lips as I leaned against the cool marble wall of the last stall, the front door squealed open. I swallowed and there it was—a sucking sensation. It's hard to describe except it's like being on the loop-the-loop of a roller coaster. There's that one second when you're upside down and the centrifugal—or is it centripetal?—force yanks your head back even though gravity wants to pull it downwards. It's kind of like that. I noticed for the first time that my clothes shrank down as well, slits forming in my overalls for the wings and extra legs, as if the cloth were in collusion with my body. My eyes fractured like two rose windows and I could see everywhere around the girls bathroom, even behind me to a spot where a spider beckoned with her undulating legs, the bitch.

The girls were discussing me. They parsed out rolls for my next victimization via dodge ball. The idea had something to do with pelting my body with all the red rubber balls kept in a bin near our classroom door. Instead of sticking around to hear more, I buzzed out the window and back inside an open window into our classroom, which was void of children—everyone was playing at recess, our teacher no doubt smoking and gossiping in the lounge with her colleagues. In the coatroom, I found the girls' lunchboxes, some carelessly left open from our snack hour. I proceeded to spit into their sandwiches, Twinkies and Thermoses. I even managed a crap on Dina Miller's apple. And that girl loved her apples, snarfling down to the core like a barn-raised sow. I turned back into a little girl and, using my teacher's permanent marker, wrote in Jerry Lofton's dyslexic handwriting: I'M AN OINKER on all the girls' windbreakers. Feeling sorry for Jerry isn't necessary. He liked to hold girls down behind the library and stick his hand inside their panties, telling them he was going to marry them. I learned to avoid wearing dresses and skirts because of Jerry.

• • •

It wasn't until high school that I gained control over it. Love helped.

I admit, I spied often in high school. Don't judge; you would too. I only did what anyone else in my position would do—scalping answer keys to math tests I was sure to fail, flying in just before last bell (I rarely carried a bag to and from school. Copying homework answers off my peers proved to be a piece of cake. I may be lazy, but I have excellent short-term memory). The usual, unimaginative stuff. I was still a weirdo with no real friends. But who needs friends when you can know everything about anyone you want just by digging in your sticky toes and hanging upside down?

Who needs friends? I do—or did.

I was in love with Juan Garcia, and he was in love with Jeannie Blake. That part was fine—they were like soap opera stars, in a league of their own looks-wise. I just wanted to watch them, like daytime television.

That's not entirely true. If they had offered to take me under their wings, I would have wept for joy. I followed them home from school one day like Mary's little lamb. They went into his house, and I thought, if I can't be with Juan, at least I could be a fly on the wall of his room. So I did it: I turned. As per usual, my clothes shrank around my tiny body and my feet left the ground. I slipped through a crack under the back door and zipped around corners, following their voices, their smells. My senses become stronger when I'm a fly (I bet you all love that, don't you?), and Juan's scent was potent—grilled cheese and Right Guard. Outside the door to his bedroom, I paused, listening to the hum of their conversation. I don't know what I expected. I'd never had sex, had only seen its rudimentary portrayal in the made-for-TV movies my mother liked to watch. I guess I was expecting live porn. Would they have exchanged pieces of clothing? Perhaps he was wearing her bra. Maybe he had a leather-and-lace fetish, or a thing for uncorked wine bottles, or maybe he just liked it straight. The door wasn't completely closed. I flew inside.

They were sitting on his bed, which was neatly made. I found a good spot in the corner to observe their foreplay, but no such thing—unless talking about AIDS is sexy. That was literally the topic of the day; we had just had some "alternative lifestyles" guest speakers at school assembly that morning, specifically, a lesbian and a gay man. Some genius had asked during Q and A if either of them had AIDS. Jeannie was arguing that it had been a legitimate question. Juan kept shaking his head and saying, "It's messed up. It's just messed up." I waited around for an hour, but they didn't do anything else. There were some awkward silences between them. Finally, Jeannie left. Since I knew boys had the reputation for being rather large horn-dogs, I expected that Juan would at least take off his shirt and have some "alone time" after all that talk and no action. But he simply sat at his desk and pulled out his homework. He might have been easy on the eyes, but I found him rather boring.

Still, I held out hope. After he'd done his work, he lay down on the bed with a surfing magazine, but soon nodded off. I flew under his box spring and turned back into a girl. I whispered in his ear, "Love Musette. She's the perfect girl for you." He stirred, and I flew away home.

The next day, he asked me out. We went to a movie and then to the cool-kids' hang: the break room of the Coronet Cinema where he and the rest of the football team worked after school and weekends. My presence shocked everyone. I know because I spied on them whenever I could. But all I had to do was visit him in his sleep every now and then and remind him in my drone: "Musette is the one."

I rode his coattails and we were voted prom king and queen. We slept together that summer and I had my first orgasm with him—he wasn't so boring after all. At the end of the summer, we promised to remain faithful during college, but he stopped calling and writing within two weeks. In the winter, his family moved to Scottsdale, Arizona, then I heard to some place in New Mexico, and Juan Garcia disappeared from my life.

• • •

College is usually where the weirdos break out of their chrysalis, but not me. I remained weird and alone. I still lived at home, like any good Asian offspring. My mother cooked for me and did my laundry with little complaint. I went to classes, kept in the top ten percent (but you probably know all this, don't you?). I got my first fake ID and hightailed it to the Rotten Rottweiller, my college's see-and-be-seen bar. Men began to approach me. I found if I stared at them, and rolled my shoulder muscles just a little, it produced a faint, hypnotic hum that drew them in—like bees to honey. I got plenty of dates with drunken frat boys as well as a few grizzled barflies, who will sleep with nearly anything when schnozzled. Once, I even got pregnant. It was a simple matter of changing into fly-form and laying the eggs under some eucalyptus leaves in the park. Sometimes I wonder how they're doing, my children.

• • •

Once, an old lady tried to keep me as a pet. She lived in my grandfather's apartment building. I'd brought him some *dan tat*, the Chinese egg custards he loves so much, and after our visit, decided to fly home—it was faster than three cross-town bus transfers. A door opened and an unexpected draft carried me into the lady's home. She called me

Flora and left a dish of non-dairy creamer for me. She told me about her children who had died when the Yangtze flooded. They were still alive in her mind, playing in the yard, going to school. "They'll come home soon," she said. "They just went for a swim. Good exercise." But then she remembered that the current had been too powerful, that they were gone, and she would grieve for hours, her sobs turning to endless trickles. Eventually, she grew careless. She opened a window to empty her ashtray in the alley below and I zoomed out into the fresh air, free.

• • •

I know why you people contacted me. And I know this application is a mere formality, that you would snap me up in a heartbeat. And I know why being a beautiful butterfly is out of the question. How else could I blend? Disappearing into my common housefly guise is essential to what you want from me and to what gives me the most satisfaction in life. But you see, freedom suits me.

When I saw your woman—in pink, not black, although the sunglasses at night were a nice touch—I knew right off. Was it just a coincidence that I had just mailed off a batch of graduate school applications? It's a mishmash of stuff—journalism school, vet school, law school. I like to keep my options open.

Well, who would have thought cosmetology school? Hair? Skin care? Snooping? Sure, why not—it's the perfect front. Who *doesn't* confide to their stylist—and the strangest things! Of course, I've been waiting for this, have known you'd come around sooner or later. No—sooner, before I'm too old. And I'm not scared of you, although you pretend not to menace, I know you *would* hurt a fly. You'd have to swat me first, and that will never happen. I'm too fast and too wary—my father didn't die for nothing.

Sure. Since meeting that woman, I've tried to imagine what academy life would be like—I know, I know, you claim it's just beauty school. Beauty by day, commando by night, right? I must confess I have little curiosity about those who are like me. We'd probably have group therapy sessions over henna treatments or tea socials to compare notes on our "situation" as fellow freaks.

You know what? I just realized that I'm wasting my time, sitting in this windowless room with the little camera on the wall—yes, I know it's there behind that ugly sconce—watching me the way I watch the world. Sorry, but I'm going to pass on your—yes, I'll admit it—your rather flattering offer; however, I will finish this essay and tell you why. In my aloneness, I am special. Because, you see, I am just an ordinary woman. Almost offensively average. My ability, gift, abnormality, whatever you want to call it, if given to another more innovative—more *motivated*—person might do you and our country some actual good. If I had to be around those who actually put whatever it is they have to good use, I'm not sure I could bear the competition.

Besides, what has it ever really done for me? Did it win me friends? Did it find me love? Because that's all I've ever wanted. It's silly, I know, but the life of a fly isn't that long. My father, a young man, was just a little older than I am when he died. An accident, I know, but no one can tell me if longevity is to be my paternal trademark—my mother says he was an orphan, and never knew his family. Who knows how much time I have left to eat picnic crumbs. To coerce young lads into holding me in their arms, even for one night. To skim along a thermal. To amuse myself by clinging to a wall and learning the secret wishes of your heart.

MIKI HSU LEAVEY
DEDICATION

Hisako Hibi, artist

To my good friend, Hisako Hibi: In her life-
time, she was a single mother of four, a survivor of internment policies during WWII,
a young widow and a celebrated Japanese
painter recognized by presidents and the
Smithsonian Institute. She was as wise as she
was influential, as humble as she was powerful. As a young painter she recorded her
suffering and that of her people on canvas
during the imprisonment of the Japanese
in America. As a mature painter, her work
underwent radical change, moving towards
abstraction and subtlety. Every simple conversation I had with her was mind breaking. When I was newly pregnant for the first
time, while I was distressed and unsure about
whether I could sustain a life as an artist, she
gently pulled me aside and whispered in
her demure Japanese way, "Miki, don't worry. I painted. I survived. The world of the
mother is a wonderful thing. I feel sorry
for women who think that to be an artist, they should not have children. They do
not know what they are missing. There will
be days when you must not pick up your
brush because your child is sick or hungry.
There will be many days when you will not
be needed. Keep your brush and have your
child." She passed away nearly twenty years
after she took me under her wing. She was
the only person I have known who could
quickly cross an open field without ever
seeming to run.

MIKI HSU LEAVEY
Obscuring Music. Mixed media on paper, 30" x 22"

MariNaomi
Dedication

Yoko Ono, performance, installation artist
I would like to dedicate my work to the amazing and vibrant Yoko Ono. As a half-Japanese girl growing up in a predominantly Caucasian environment, my classmates teased me and called me "Yoko." I disliked this comparison, as her name was frequently associated with the breakup of The Beatles. Over time I learned more about her, her courage, tenacity, genius and innovation, eventually making her a personal hero of mine. Her example has driven me to always push forward and try new things, regardless of how they may affect others' opinions of me. If someone compared me to her now I'd be nothing but flattered. Yoko Ono rocks.

MariNaomi
Cruelty to Animals. Mixed media, 53" x 21"

GAYLE MAK
DEDICATION

Catalina Cariaga, poet

Filipina–American poet, Catalina Cariaga, is
the author of *Cultural Evidence* and *E Pluri-
bus Karaoke*. Her poetry, part of a growing
body of acclaimed Filipina-American writing, examines her family's diaspora from the
Southeast Asian Pacific Islands to California, exploring themes of displacement,
cross-cultural confusion and what it means
to be Filipina-American. I first discovered
Cariaga when I came across her poem,
"Plantings," in a poetry anthology. Her
poem captured my imagination with its
skillful word craft and the themes of food,
immigrant identities, parental sacrifice and
cross-cultural negotiations. As a writer,
I find Cariaga's fresh treatment of these
familiar themes and her innovative exploration of language very inspiring.

WORKSHOPPING i
GAYLE MAK

i am in danger
of losing my
i   been
told to scram, get
lost, make way, dis
guise as some
thing else as
i t, some trendier
i.d., even
moi, just don't be
brown
tweed suit wearing
i that says
i lack imagination
lack ambition lack
ability to defy
predictions define
taste
too personal i that gets too
scarily intimate too
confessional in your face so
i should be
dumping
i embarrassing i
that can't pronounce
in no va tion
spell brilliant
deploy wit

understand
genius
is not
an adjective
but a motive
dictate cutting
edge that
dictates
i has to go
without knowing
what that leaves us or
what to do with
i's
bastard child
me

JOAN MAEDA TRYGG
DEDICATION

Mitsuye Yamada, poet

I grew up in one of the predominantly white suburbs of St. Paul, Minnesota. I had never thought about how being of Japanese descent shaped my sense of who I was in the world, until I was nearly thirty years old and my sister gave me a copy of Mitsuye Yamada's essay, *Invisibility is an Unnatural Disaster: Reflections of an Asian American Woman*. I was stunned that the experience of not being seen was shared by other women, and that what lay behind it was our Japanese faces. Yamada's writings—*Desert Run* and *Camp Notes*— showed me that my life and history, though not found in my school history books, were significant, and rich ground from which to write. I owe Mitsuye Yamada a great debt for opening the door to the world of women of color, the world where I am no longer invisible.

THE FAMILY CAR
JOAN MAEDA TRYGG

The first car I remember was a two-toned 1958 Dodge Coronet, a car I felt close to because it was born nearly the same year as I. It was turquoise and white, with fins and whitewall tires. Inside, it had a beige ceiling and a hump. I thought the humps were for standing on, as I did, leaning against the front seat and peering out the windshield between my parents' heads. I remember standing on the hump and eating a Milky Way, when Dad hit a bump. The Milky Way smashed into the ceiling, leaving a chocolate mark that stayed with the car until it was junked. But Dad tells me it wasn't me with the candy bar, but Janet, my older sister, and I'm inclined to believe his adult memory over my child one. After all, it was his car, and he's always taken excellent care of his cars.

Back in those days, there were no mandatory seat belt or car seat laws, and on long trips, my parents installed a platform that transformed the back seat into a level playing area. I remember the scratchy logan army blanket Mom spread for us to play on. Sometimes, on our way home from weekly grocery shopping at Foodtown, we rode in the trunk. No one looking at the car knew we were there in the enclosing darkness, curled around the spare tire that was bolted to the floor, grocery bags of cold meat, canned goods and produce resting against our backs. We giggled as we talked and cracked candy necklaces between our teeth. When Janet's Girl Scout troop had paper drives, we sat on bundles of newspapers bound in twine, with the trunk open. I watched the suburban lawns recede behind us as we bumped slowly along, the asphalt road close enough I could see small stones embedded in it, the smell of oil and exhaust, newsprint and twine filling my nostrils. It was those newspapers that eventually broke the springs on that car.

The Dodge had double headlights, one large bulb on top of the other, and yellow parking lights set closer to the center. The car smiled at me with golden eyeteeth. My dad does not have golden eyeteeth, yet the face of the car seemed to me to be the face of my dad. We would watch for his face to come over the hill at 6:15 in the evening. When it crested the hill, half a block away, we would run and hide in the closet in the entryway. When he came in the door, we jumped out and yelled, "boo!" Every night, he was surprised to see us.

• • •

I learned to drive in a maroon 1967 Mustang. When I was in high school, I didn't see much of Dad. He worked long hours, waking me up on his way out the door, and returning home just before I went to bed. But he taught me how to drive, and took me out for practice. I looked forward to the hour or so when he would be my captive audience. I felt comfortable talking with my dad, more than I did with my mom at that time, the darkness around us and our eyes on the road. I don't remember what we talked about, only feeling happy and companionable and relaxed, with the road unwinding beneath my wheels.

I thought the car was cool. It had black bucket seats, and the stick was on the floor, though it was an automatic. One night, when my sister came out of the grocery store where she worked, the car was gone. The police found it undamaged a few days later, with a half tank of gas still in it. I wished it could tell us all of its adventures. The first New Year's Eve I drove, I picked up some friends and went to a party. The new year ushered in bitter Minnesota temperatures below zero, and with five or six of us in the car, frost quickly sealed us into opaqueness. I couldn't figure out how to turn on the defroster, so I drove everyone home with the windows wide open.

Dad always took Sundays off of work. Nearly every week, we would pile into the big station wagon, a 1969 Plymouth Custom Suburban. My sisters and I sat in the middle seat. Donna, the youngest of the three, sat in the center; Janet and I by the windows. Our two younger brothers sat in the way back, where the seat faced backwards. A few years ago, my youngest brother, David, confessed to hating the way back seat, where he could only see where we had been. We listened to music we had taped from the radio: the Carpenters, John Denver,

Johnny Cash. We drove to Lake Pepin on the Mississippi River between Minnesota and Wisconsin, perhaps ate a picnic lunch, played softball and threw river-smooth pebbles into the lake. On our way, we watched for license plates from other states and counted Volkswagens, Mustangs, Dusters and other cars we could recognize. Dad told me how Buicks always had three vents on the sides. He didn't tell Janet, and she was amazed that I could recognize Buicks. When we drove through the country, we counted cows. They had to be on your own side of the car. Cows counted a point apiece, white horses counted ten, and black horses subtracted ten. If we passed a cemetery on your side, you lost all your points. Sometimes Dad would go around the corner so the cemetery would be on Janet's side instead of mine.

• • •

The first car my dad drove was a 1936 Plymouth that belonged to his dad. He'd been driving it for a year when they had to sell it. You couldn't have cars at Minidoka, where they were interned in 1942. He sold it to a friend, who would drive it to visit him in the assembly center at Puyallup, where Dad and his family stayed before going to Minidoka. I appreciated his visits, Dad said, but it was awfully hard to watch him drive away in that car. In 1991, Dad, along with all the other former internees still living, received a letter of apology from the government and a check for $20,000. He spent part of it on a 1992 Honda Civic CX, in which he and my mom took many trips. Sometimes some combination of my siblings and I traveled with them, and we still looked for license plates, though we never counted cows. Dad pointed out old cars and asked if we knew what they were. New Buicks don't have vents, so I've lost my edge; Donna knows far

Nakazato LaFreniere
Dedication

Roshni Rustomji, historian, writer

Roshni Rustomji, a historian, reads original Spanish documents from colonial Latin America to recover Asian American history in the colonial Americas. Despite the myth that Asians did not come into the Americas until the Gold Rush, Rustomji has examined the history of people, like Mirrha/Catarina de San Juan, a visionary/slave/healer, who entered Mexico between the 1500s and 1700s with others on the Manila-Acapulco route. As the Asian settling of the Americas has always been from the West Coast moving eastward, the importance of studying Asians in colonial Spanish territories, which included the Latin American countries, California, Arizona, New Mexico, Texas and others, is essential in understanding the earliest Asian American settlers from slaves like Mirrha/Catarina and Juan de Zumarraga to Chinese barbers and Filipino rebels. Rustomji has lectured at American universities on Mirrha/Catarina, opening the awareness of her audience to the experience of one woman who was among the first wave of settlers. Mirrha came here in 1620 at about age eleven, having been kidnapped by pirates and sold into slavery, and later becoming a devout Catholic. Writings survive to this time of her healing touch that brought people to her door. When she died, her Jesuit priest applied to Rome to make her a saint but the Inquisition ordered her biographies burned instead. Luckily, not all the biographies were burned and a dedicated historian was able to read the original text that recorded her visions and confessions to her priest.

more cars than I do. Riding together gave us an opportunity to talk. Dad and Mom told stories and remembered things that didn't come out when we were at home. Sometimes they were small things: Mom remembering how she held a knife between her knees and quartered potatoes on it, Dad remembering the sand in the kelp Grandma gathered and dried to eat. Other times, they filled in family history I had never heard before. Dad talked about how he and Grandma had been hit by a truck when he was six, putting him in a body cast for months, and years later, disqualifying him for military service during WWII. Maybe there's something about heading back to the places they were raised. Maybe there's something about being enclosed together, separated from the rest of the world in a bubble of steel and glass, the road unwinding beneath us. Something about shared histories and creating new stories. Something about connection, about having time for each other.

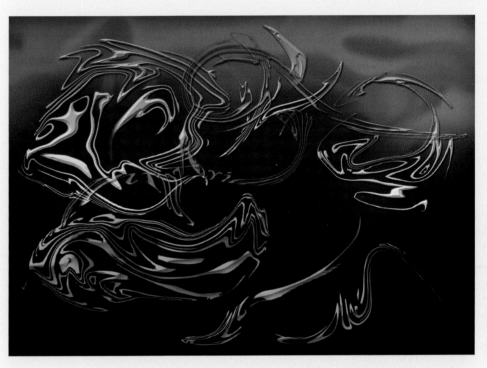

Lolan Buhain Sevilla
Dedication

Margarita Alcantara-Tan, writer, publisher

Never in my life have I fit into any type of Pilipina feminine ideal. Growing up I struggled to find a community that could hold the complexity of my identities: Pinay, queer, politically radical, artist, butch, tattooed, vocal. Isolated doesn't quite capture the loneliness I experienced, but it sure does come close. One year I came across a 'zine called *Bamboo Girl* by Margarita Alcantara-Tan, a culturally and politically charged publication that validated the existence of nontraditional Asian women. Her courage to acknowledge and challenge notions of the taboo helped destigmatize topics like mental health and queerness, adding to the mix articles on Pilipino folklore, martial arts and indigenous culture. Holding her writing in my hand and eagerly awaiting the next issue, I found a model for putting pen to paper. Writing became accessible, my voice and experience just as sacred. Finding that model influenced my process as a writer, shut down those voices of self-doubt and brought to the forefront my desire to use art and culture towards social change without compromising any of my identities.

The Redolence of Brown Erotic
Lolan Buhain Sevilla

i.

in the land of my ancestors

faces all hues of brown

piqued curiosity

at ours

somehow sensing

we were the same

yet still different

their stares weren't invasive

just respectful

and honest

like i prayed them to be

my mama told me

they'll be able to smell your american

i didn't know how to understand

until i stepped foot

into welcome arms

motherland

a million lifetimes away

never seemed like home

until now

my senses adjusting

pilipino smelled different

at the center than it did in the margins

each second my universe expanded

translating the scents of new brown

jeepney exhaust with

fried chicken stands on the corner

of rojas and united nations boulevard

the rain tasted of bitter tears

on asphalt cheeks

bayan is the word used to describe

community, land and folks

all at the same time

america never smelled like this

ii.

i always woke at 4 am

the low hum of air conditioning

blowing curtains above our heads

kept me company

the damp light of wind and rain

poking through

shadowed your face

you never knew i'd watch you sleep

let my heart burst bright for you

every start of a new day

your lolo's house sleeping in quiet approval

i was made to love you

your body curved into mine

like 7000 islands

fit perfect in legacy

this

was the first time

i truly understood

the significance

of two pinays in love

it was never lost on me

the blessing of you

and this trip

spirits taking steps alongside

acquainting us

with one another

layer

underneath

layer

until i could see what it was

i had written

upon the underside of your soul

and it didn't matter

the kisses we had to sneak in corners

while heads were turned

or the language we created

to say 'i love you'

while in the presence of others—

did you know then

that you

as well

were made to love me?

iii.

one night

after three san miguel premiums

got me tipsy enough

to say

what fear of the unknown

held me back from boldly proclaiming

you stepped to me with reassurance

and said

baby, we're in the philippines

and this became the moment defined

a resolution sharp memory

when the color brown

synthesized

into sound and touch

my lips found your face

kissed lightly

every contour

waiting to be

savored

my baby's sweat tasted sweeter

at the nape of her neck

my tongue

collecting each drop

with the precision of an alchemist

careful not to skip an inch

i found the exact circular motion

to draw your breath

rapid and full

sex in complete darkness
when you have to feel your way around
one another's body
the humidity drenched rawness
bringing out fuck pheromones
dormant until now
spun me crazy
as fingers, tongues and fists
worked their frenzied magic
bringing moans
that had to be stifled
by pillows and hands

you bit into my skin
brown as the blood
that pumps your heart
alive
rode me
grinding until the bed soaked
from pussy juice sweat tears

that night
the winds howled for us
scared geckos into the cracks of ceilings
as we lay drenched
much like the hanging laundry outside
trying to dry despite november rains
this was just round one
i read in your eyes
could still feel your hunger
as fingertips traced circles
around my nipples
the taste of chocolate
puckering
waiting to engulf your mouth
sacred as this land holding spirits
that night we bore one another
christened ourselves warriors
this
the redolence of brown erotic

AMY LAM
DEDICATION

Golda Supanova, singer, songwriter

The power to transform a placid audience into frenetic madness is a power reserved for white commercialized pop stars, or larger-than-life divas from abroad. Or so I once thought, until I witnessed Golda Supanova perform her revelatory brand of rock music for the first time. Here was a mother of two, an original singer-songwriter, who could bend an audience to her will, smashing every preconceived notion I ever had about what an Asian American diva should be. Eyes rolled back, twirling semicircles with a microphone stand, her voice and words infuse passion into our bodies. Only recently Golda released a full-length CD titled "Lava Flow," although she has been a Bay Area APA rock star for years, on the verge of smashing out of the underground scene. Every time I see Golda perform, I watch her with envy as she grips a crowd with a power I will never possess.

MAY LEE
DEDICATION

Mai Neng Moua, writer, publisher

I would like to dedicate my submission to Mai Neng Moua, a Hmong woman and writer who has been pivotal to the Hmong literary movement. As a college student, she started the journal, *Paj Ntaub Voice*, which has survived after ten years and has now spawned a literary magazine. She inspired not only me but other writers to succeed through creating a space where our voices could be heard. She is also an activist in daring us to write ourselves into existence as opposed to letting others control images of who we are.

FARMER'S MARKET
MAY LEE

You always see her there
A small figure hidden behind the
zaub ntsuab, green onions, and bell peppers
We pass by in tank tops and shorts
while she is forever bundled in a thick jacket
to ward off the sun
Despite her best efforts
He has touched her face
Imbedding creases around
eyes that used to laugh
a mouth that used to pierce hearts
Her jerky-textured skin
has long forgotten a lover's touch
Her head, wrapped in a bright handkerchief
Splattered with flowers,
hides thinning, permed hair
that has died at her shoulders
Her hands no longer need the protection of gloves
They have built immunity to the pricks and stings of work
Every week, she comes to sell vegetables
Aware she is not in the market anymore
She plays the grandma
the niam tais who sends familiar
greetings to young patrons
But sometimes
In the solitude of her truck
In the empty fields of her crops
In the darkness of the night
Laying in her sole twin bed
She remembers being loved

AMY LAM

Madonna of Asia. Installation, 30" x 36" x 18". *Photo by Ed Osada.*

TERRY ACEBO DAVIS
DEDICATION

Dawn Nakanishi, metalsmith, installation artist

Dawn Nakanishi is a "light" to those that know her as: teacher, mentor, artist, sister, friend, swimmer and cancer survivor. I have known her since art graduate school. An accomplished metalsmith (jeweler), teacher/artist, she has taught her craft to thousands of students; many are now trade colleagues. Her artwork is personal and universal. She takes forms from nature and sculpts them in metal, creating a new meaning and relevance. In her installations, Dawn uses river boulders and water elements to create spaces for reflection, meditation and healing.

As a child, Dawn was coached by her father to be a competitive swimmer. I believe this competitive spirit was the healing force in her determination to fight breast cancer. Through her hard work and optimism, Dawn slayed the dragon. She will always be an inspiration to me and to those who are fortunate to meet her.

TERRY ACEBO DAVIS
Aguila. Serigraph, 40" x 32"

TAMIKO BEYER
DEDICATION

Mitsuye Yamada, poet

I came across the work of Japanese American poet Mitsuye Yamada when I was in college and looking for other poets whose voices resonated with me, who had experiences I could relate to, who wrote in ways that were different from the poets of the canon that I had always been exposed to. I was captured by the immediacy of her language, how she unfolded stories within the poetic form, how she used language and silence as a form of resistance. Yamada became an inspiration to me, and for the first time I realized that I was part of a tradition of Japanese American women poets. That was an incredibly powerful realization and continues to help me place my work in a meaningful context today.

SETAGAYA-KU HAIBUN
FALL 1982, TOKYO
TAMIKO BEYER

Gingko trees cast off their fruit—sour stink rising from rotten ghosts. The white line dividing sidewalk from road is stained brown, stained slick by the globes. I am eight, my loafers marvelous with their fake American pennies. I crush laced exoskeletons under my soles—cicadas grown so large they burst from their skins: now shells, air. Detritus among lost bobby pins and sick, soft fruit. Since the first cold snap, the nights hang silent, gaping where they once *sh sh shimmered*, brushed by a thousand wings. On the other side of the tall wall saturated by late afternoon light, college boys laugh, bounce tennis balls against stone. The street is an empty tongue. I imagine stepping past the white line, edging into the wide, calling street.

If a car turned, would
it find my body soft, as
crushable as fruit?

TERRY ACEBO DAVIS
My Anak Tableaux (detail). Mixed media

STEPHANIE HAN
DEDICATION

Maxine Hong Kingston, writer

I was fifteen when I first read Maxine Hong Kingston's book *The Woman Warrior.* The book made me rethink my ideas of what an Asian American woman could be. It was literature that spoke to my desires, writing that portrayed an Asian American character I could fully embrace. In the throes of those pages I was no longer an adolescent captive in the suburbs, aching for escape and yearning for acceptance, but a dreamer, a fighter, a writer and an artist.

THE LADIES OF SHEUNG WAN

STEPHANIE HAN

She couldn't take another step.

Maybe I'll just stop for a moment, Yuk Ki said to herself. Just sit, right here. She didn't. She knew what would happen if she sat down on the steps by the exit of the neon-lit café in Sheung Wan filled with people in clean clothes. More than that, if she sat, she was giving in. She looked down the street: Che Sum was nowhere in sight. She leaned against her handcart and tried to shut out the noise from the city.

With bowled legs shaped like a bent iron magnet and a spine so curved it forced her to look at the ground, she had to twist her neck like a turtle to see. Most of the time, Yuk Ki didn't care; she knew the way they looked at her pushing her handcart stacked with cardboard—this was just life. It wasn't her fault her son died. Yes, she had thrown her daughter out of the house, but at the time Moy was nothing but trouble and besides, it had been ten years since Moy had left Hong Kong. She was in Canada. Children don't do what they should for their parents. Didn't matter. She got on fine by herself.

Years ago, she and Ming Ho sold newspapers; they even had their own stand by Wing On department store when business was really booming, but the stand went bust. The 7-11's really killed them. Who wanted to buy a newspaper from old people on a corner when you could get it at 7-11? By the time Ming Ho died, they were back where they started, out on the street, sitting on the cement steps down from Cat's Alley with a stack of newspapers and an old basket of coins. Back then she and Ming Ho would talk to Che Sum whenever she passed them. The three would take a quick break and then Che Sum would be off, pushing her handcart down the street.

Collecting cardboard for recycling was hard work, but after Ming Ho died, Che Sum had helped her get a handcart and showed her what cardboard pieces were best, how to stack and tie everything properly so things wouldn't slip off. Lean and wiry, Yuk Ki was ten years Che Sum's senior but she managed to push the load up Wellington from Queen's Road, right past that fancy new gym, slow to be sure, but she made it like everybody else. Lately, the junction seemed steeper; it took longer to get around the curve. The slight slope was like a long steep hill and she found herself taking a break on the cement island in the middle of the road waiting for lights to change red-green-red-green-red-green, massaging the back of her neck with her stiff hands, before she finally shoved off to move the handcart. People never liked it when she stood there for too long; women shuddered and shrank away, fearful their skirts would brush her. When they looked, men said, get out of the way old woman.

—You get out of the way, she'd answer defiantly behind her cart. You'd smell like garbage too, if you spent your days picking from the dumps, she wanted to say but never did. Drivers honked when she didn't cross the street fast enough, but they never hit, at least not her.

She and Che Sum were meeting up as they often did, to exchange news or eat rice together. Yuk Ki waved when she saw Che Sum down the block and watched her navigate the cart through the narrow street between taxicabs.

—Lots of boxes. People moving in that new building, said Che Sum. We can go back after lunch. Hot today. Hey, sit down.

—I'll sit, said Yuk Ki. She didn't sit but stood looking at the crowd. Lunchtime. Everyone was hungry, rushing to eat, impatient to get back to work. She was hungry.

Now and then the two women worked together, but more often than not, they each spent their day alone. It was hot, the weather had turned and the chill had left the air. The wet heat clung to their bodies and hung in the air like layers of steam. The city was waiting for the monsoons, summer rains to wash away the grime—the spit on the sidewalks, the dust from construction, the stench of car fumes and garbage.

—Shoes look good, said Che Sum.

—Comfortable. High quality. These will last a long time, said Yuk Ki.

Yuk Ki was finally comfortable in the shoes Che Sum had retrieved from the dump by the new apartment complex on Queen's Road. Che Sum had presented Yuk Ki

with the new footwear after watching her friend slip on a rainy day.

—Slippers are fine, but us old women need all the help we can get, Che Sum had told Yuk Ki. Take off your slippers. Here. These are almost new.

—These are kids' shoes.

—Just be glad they're not the kind with the flashing red light on the back. Those would be good, though. Especially when it gets dark.

—Nothing wrong with my slippers.

—Old woman, don't be silly. Here, wear the shoes. Don't tell me I spent all that time digging them out of the dump and you're not going to wear them!

When Yuk Ki's back started hurting more, Che Sum had said that they should work as a team. They both knew that it would mean less money, though now and then when it came out the same, Che Sum casually said that it was more profitable to work together. Yuk Ki put up a protest so as not to appear needy and Che Sum said what was proper, that Yuk Ki was doing the favor when it was really the other way around.

Yuk Ki hesitated before the stoop of the Sheung Wan café and then eased her bottom onto the step.

—Good idea, said Che Sum. Sit down. We need a short break. Too much work. Oh, the heat is bad today. Work slow. That's best. I'll get something to drink. What do you want?

—Water, said Yuk Ki.

—Wait right here, said Che Sum. She scuttled across the street and came back with a bottle of water.

—Here, said Che Sum. I told you, sit down. Sit down! Right here on the step. Che Sum pulled out a handkerchief from her pocket and dabbed Yuk Ki's forehead. Yuk Ki shifted her posture; she slumped her shoulders, closed her eyes, and patted Che Sum's hand.

—I'm fine. Just sitting for a minute. So hot today, said Yuk Ki. Sure, the manager might try to push them, maybe dump water on them, who knows, but it wouldn't be for a while. They could afford to sit.

—Yes, let's take a rest, agreed Che Sum.

The café manager came out and started to yell.

—Get off old woman! Get off!

Che Sum growled right back, ready to scowl at anyone who dared to take a sidelong glance at Yuk Ki.

—Don't worry, Yuk Ki, just take a breath, said Che Sum, patting her on the shoulder. Yuk Ki nodded, sweating in the noonday heat as her hand gripped the wall. You just sit—rest, said Che Sum, her gruff voice softened with worry.

The manager went back inside. Yuk Ki glanced at her friend's navy blue flowered shirt, black cotton pants and fabric shoes and looked down at her own equally dirty pair. Two old women, that's what we are, like shriveled pieces of dried ginger. Che Sum is younger, but still an old woman. The police were sure to tell them to move along. Bastards. No respect for elders.

There was the day a woman had shouted for them to get out of the dumpster, called them names. Usually Che Sum yelled back or ignored people but young Che Sum didn't fight back. Old Yuk Ki had stepped in.

—Leave us alone! Stupid woman, said Yuk Ki. Squawk. Squawk. You sound like a chicken!

—Let's go, said Che Sum.

—That building's a waste of time. Don't listen to her, said Yuk Ki. Forget it. Let's go eat. Forget about that squawking woman.

Che Sum was quiet.

Everyone gets tired. Who would look after her friend, Che Sum? Silly really, she's the one who watches me, thought Yuk Ki.

—You sit, said Che Sum. That fool's always like that.

—Maybe five minutes, said Yuk Ki. She didn't want to sit. But it was hot.

Che Sum nodded. She touched Yuk Ki's spotted gnarled hands. Yuk Ki pressed her deep brown cheek against the cool of the mint green tile. People passed and someone spit near their feet. When the café door swung open and patrons spilled out, the welcome draft of chilly air quickly disappeared.

—So hot, said Yuk Ki letting the heat push her down. It didn't seem so bad to give in a little. What would she have ever done without Che Sum? Even now, working together —Che Sum could do better on her own.

—You just sit, said Che Sum, fanning her friend. The rain's coming.

The warm rain began to fall and the steps became slick with water. Yuk Ki looked at Che Sum's hot and sticky face and smiled. Che Sum—a good friend. Like a sister.

—How can I worry about five years from now if I can't figure out five hours from now, Che Sum had always told Yuk Ki.

—You're young, Yuk Ki had said, emphasizing her seniority. You need to think about the future. At my age, it's different. Che Sum had brushed the comment aside, younger people didn't listen.

Yuk Ki slowly sipped water from the bottle.

—Stay right there, Che Sum said, looking at her friend. You need to rest. I'll cover the cardboard. Che Sum got up and began covering the stacked cardboard with strips of black and clear plastic, garbage and grocery bags cut in half, woven vinyl tarps of blue and red stripes.

Yuk Ki agreed. A little rest might be good. Doesn't mean anything. Just five minutes. The café customers were carefully stepping around them but Yuk Ki's eyes were closed. All she could hear were the jackhammer voices collapsing into the sounds of the street.

—She's getting sick right here. You need to do something about this scum, ruining my business, the manager yelled to the policeman across the street. The policeman ignored him until a few people began to block the narrow sidewalk.

—The old woman's dying. Get the ambulance.

—What's happening?

—Get those carts out of the road, old woman.

—Drive around them, Che Sum barked to the driver. You rest, she told Yuk Ki.

—Yes, whispered Yuk Ki. She felt her heart rapidly beating. She wanted to reassure her friend. Young Che Sum shouldn't worry, she looked so small and frail. Yuk Ki wanted to speak, but settled for squeezing Che Sum's hand.

Che Sum huddled next to her, silently weeping as she fanned Yuk Ki with a fan of torn cardboard. As the slight wind of the fan hit her forehead Yuk Ki thought of the day on the ferry, tiny Moy wrapped in a blanket. The wind skipped off the harbor and Moy wriggled and smiled.

—It's going to be fine. Yuk Ki, Yuk Ki! Don't worry, don't worry. I'll take care of the cart, Che Sum cried.

People were shouting and strangers had gathered. The policeman stood nearby but Che Sum rocked Yuk Ki in her arms, holding her close and sobbing. A soft wind carried a few plastic bags away and the cardboard became wet, large drops of water coming down on the brown flattened boxes.

—Summer rain, that's all, Che Sum said to Yuk Ki. It's no problem, Yuk Ki. You can rest now. Just take your time.

Yes, Yuk Ki wanted to say. Don't worry, Che Sum. The slip into sleep is nothing. The relief of a warm bath. A cool drink on a hot day. The colors run blue and black behind closed eyes. Very pretty. It's all so fast. The waiting is bad—but now it's so close, so close. Nothing to fear, just a rest, she wanted to say. But she was too tired to speak.

MAY CHAN
DEDICATION

Flo Oy Wong, artist

Flo Oy Wong gives hope to artists by being a living example of "it's never too late to claim your space as an artist." She shares sage advice with any who can keep up with her speed. While she celestially globe trots, Flo is one of the down-to-earth souls of our time. To be embraced by Flo is to have a friend for life. She watches your trails and opens windows of opportunity for you. To know her is to be infected with her energy and inspired to never say never and always try your best. I admire her ability to translate our stories into her work while maintaining her responsibilities as grandmother, mother and wife. Flo is a role model for emerging artists and bearer of the torch for a global audience. Love is the center of Flo's walk and talk. I hope to always be near her light.

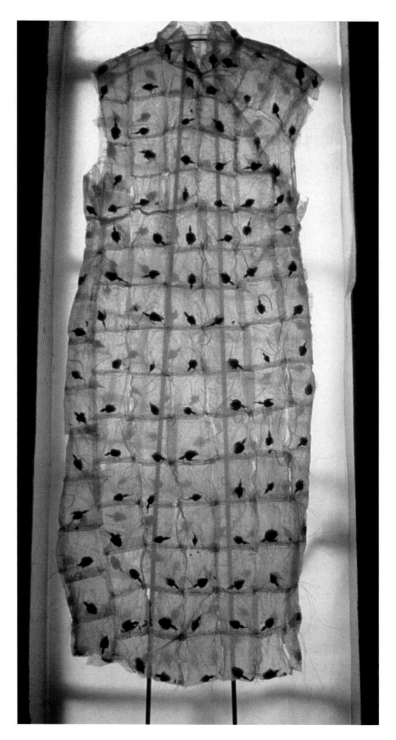

MAY CHAN
Sprout: Wither (mother's wedding dress). Rose buds, translucent tissue paper, thread, hand sewn with thread, 4.5' x 1.25'

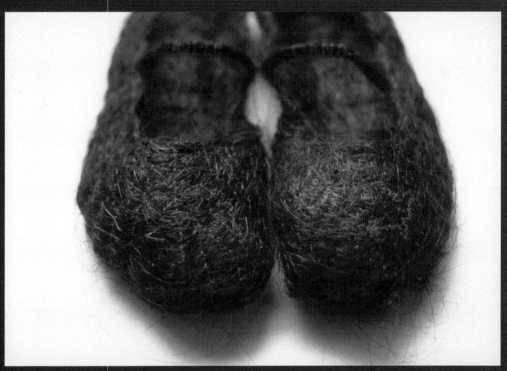

MAY CHAN

Home-Land. Hair, thread, hand woven with thread, shoe size 7.5

Dawn E. Nakanishi
Dedication

Ruth Asawa, sculptor

As a young art student, I became captivated by the sculpture of Ruth Asawa. Seeing the art of a Nisei woman prominent in the public eye was very inspiring to me. Her public art pieces throughout the San Francisco Bay Area have become the symbols and spirit of their locations and her sculptures encompass a wide variety of subject matter and technique.

In 1993, I interviewed Ruth and discovered her family was interned in the same Japanese American internment camp as my father's family. Her perseverance through racism to become an artist was very moving. She created her wire sculptures at home so her children could witness the creative process. Along with being an artist for over fifty years and a devoted mother and wife, Ruth's activism in the public shools has resulted in the children's art programs in San Francisco. Ruth Asawa is a gift in my life.

Dawn E. Nakanishi
From Darkness to Light (installation). Artist's hair, rocks, curly willow, mirror, vanity, 8' x 8' x 8'

DEBBIE YEE

DEDICATION

Josey Foo, lawyer, poet

Josey Foo is a contemporary Asian American lawyer-poet who has published two collections, *Endou* and *Tomie's Chair*, which I return to over and over again, like a dictionary or a cookbook, but for the soul. I know her work and now know her through one of my closest friends, Jenny Kim. Thus, I can report with reasonable accuracy that Josey Foo lives, writes and champions just causes in New Mexico. Her existence and her accomplishments seem to me a completely natural balance of action and serenity; and so it is both her life and her poetry which remind me not to stop writing.

BERKELEY, LATE FALL (HOMAGE TO FORREST HAMER)

DEBBIE YEE

I'd been browsing the poetry section at Cody's
—Forrest Hamer, *Berkeley, late spring*

I'd been browsing the poetry section at Cody's,

had come in to lose the unconcerned, but persistent, rain
that followed me in anyway as a trail of damp shoeprints
and dripping shoes,
wet company to a careful solitude.
I ran my right index finger across each thin spine,
flesh undulating across volume and groove,
adjusted my posture at alphabetic intervals,
imagined the bookseller coming by to fold and flatten me down
into some oblong shape and re-shelve me,
sliding face first, eyes closed into a murky sandwich
between the T's and the V's, stacked up against
the unexpected, the unknown.

And I noticed that the poems I imagined crowding around U
were a populace of the unquieted, the unrequited,
distant citizens far from the restful disposition
of the safety of S's, determinate D's, resultant R's,
where the poems are the make-believe kind,
their worlds navigable, edgeless,
unlike the bumpy, organic one I find myself wandering into.

ANN CARLI
DEDICATION

Hisako Hibi, artist

"Art consoles the spirit, and it continues on in timeless time." –Hisako Hibi

I discovered Hisako Hibi's work during a period when I had stopped writing—cold —from an accumulation of fears. I saw her paintings at the Japanese American National Museum, an exhibition of her work created during her incarceration in Topaz concentration camp in Utah during World War II. Her moving depictions of everyday life in the camps—from the laundry room to her still lifes of New Year's mochi—stunned me, both in their simplicity and their power. Hisako's paintings communicate so much about life—emotionally, practically and politically—and about the importance of art as a way to understand one's self and the world. Spending time with her paintings, made so long ago in those extreme circumstances and still able to convey her spirit, strength and humanity, gave me the courage and desire to start writing again.

THE MEASURE OF LOVE
ANN CARLI

"my dearest darling, how do i love thee? let me count the ways..." he said.

"no don't!" she said, putting her hands over her eyes. "don't show me your love with cups and spoons and lists as if love is something to be measured and sifted and doled out and mixed with this and that ingredient as if you were baking a pie or doing a sum. i want none of that."

"but babycakes! i love you more today than yesterday..." he protested.

"no no no!" she cried, blocking her ears with her palms. "there you go again, you're not listening to me. how can you compare your love from day to day? love only exists for right now. in your language what does it matter two cups today compared to one yesterday? what does it really mean? all i want is..."

"my sweet angel i just want to show you that i love you this much..." he said, opening his arms wide to enfold her.

she put her hand to her mouth and vomited on his shoes.

it was at least three cups.

FLO OY WONG

Kindred Spirit #2. Rice sack, beads, quilting, 63" x 30"
In the collection of Eleanor and Leonard Flomenhaft.

Nancy Gonzalez, librarian at the City University of New York

While teaching in New York Nancy met Helen Gee, a New York photographer and the ex-wife of Yun Gee, an avant garde artist who arrived in San Francisco in 1921 at the age of fifteen from Guangdong Province in China. During the last eight years of Helen Gee's life, Nancy became Helen's caretaker. Nancy also wrote in Chinese a recently published book about Yun Gee, a publication that introduces the Chinese-reading public to an immigrant who became a political revolutionary, cultural radical, a painter and poet in the United States. In 2005, I met Nancy when she came to California to conduct research on a new book about Asian American women artists over forty. Having inhaled Nancy's dynamic energy and vision during our brief visit, I am inspired by her commitment to tell the stories of Asian American artists.

EILEEN TABIOS
DEDICATION

Michelle Bautista, poet

Michelle Bautista is a Bay Area–based poet
and practitioner of the Filipino martial arts
known as "kali." Though she has taken poetry workshops that I've taught, I also have
taken her kali workshops. She is a master in
kali, having received 2nd place in the U.S.
national women open forms division at the
World Escrima Kali Amis Federation cham-
pionships and 3rd place in the 2000 international competition held in the Philippines.
Under her guidance, my poetry has ben-
efited from my attempts to understand kali
—specifically to be, as Michelle puts it, "like
water." This "looseness" allows things deep
in my unconscious to rise to the surface as
I write poems, thus energizing the poems in
ways that I would not have managed were I
to insist that my ego remain in control.

SUE TOM DEDICATION

Judy Kajiwara, dancer, writer, artist

I would like to dedicate my work to Judy
Kajiwara. When I first met her, she was
teaching interpretive dancing at the Japanese Cultural Community Center. Judy
follows many creative avenues: butoh dancing, creative writing, art and now has a self-
healing practice in Oakland.

Several months after my husband's passing
in 1998, I called to see if she was still teaching the dance class. Judy was no longer teaching, but she did write and shared with me
the message that came to her while she was
meditating. Her message that ended with "Be
at peace with yourself, Sue," has been a source
of strength and comfort these many years.

SUE TOM
Untitled. Raku ceramic, 24" diameter x 12" high

Ars Poetica #10,000

Eileen Tabios

Kali warriors practice
"halad"
to familiarize their bodies
with forms of martial art
so that deadly positions surface
more quickly and efficiently
during hours of war

There, gura Michelle
wields the sword
into its ten thousandth circle
within the past hour
as she prepares to battle
the jihad of alien robots
(An extra on "The Return of the Jedi,"
she cannot treat a movie as fiction
as Kali makes everything real—
just as a poem turns fiction
into truth)

If my sea petals
knew how to unfurl
I would not have been
satisfied
with sharing the same cigarette
that left your lips—

I would have gone to the source

as directly as Kali position #5—
the staff aimed directly at your pusod,
the navel symbolizing birth—

as "deeply" as the unmapped space
revealed by our meeting
choreographed by gods
whose motivations we do not know

That I compromised last night
by approximating your taste
with another drag
on an already dead cigarette

leaves the Kali practitioner
with a broken stick
and aborted movement—

leaves a circle
fragmented—

leaves a poem incomplete—

until you are ready to show me
with a "gesture"
(whose existence I know only as a rumor
and believe in only as a matter of faith):

the Poem has never asked
the poet to sacrifice Life

ANGIE CHAU
DEDICATION

Trinh Minh Ha, writer, filmmaker, composer, artist

Born in Vietnam, Trinh Minh Ha is a film-maker, writer and composer. Her films are visually stunning, intellectually rigorous and political. The way in which she explores selfhood and identity are particularly interesting to me. In *A Tale of Love*, she subverts the Vietnamese epic poem *The Tale of Kieu*, and exposes the fiction of love in love stories and the process of consumption. I like how the edges of difference rub against each other in complicated and provocative ways in Trinh Minh Ha's work. She seems to always be pushing and this inspires me to push too.

PORTRAIT OF MOTHERHOOD
ANGIE CHAU

My mother never wore a skirt past forty. She didn't want to try looking young and look like a tramp instead. My mother never wore make-up. She didn't want to appear as if she were trying, uncouth for a woman to try at all. She didn't smile often, but when she did, it was a graceful line, almost a blessing. For my first school picture, she showed me how to do the same. She showed me how to lift my lips at the corners. She showed me how to make my mouth moist. She showed me how to pout without puckering. She sat straight-backed, chin up, hands resting on her lap. But when I smiled, my lips parted. She said, "Remember, a lady never exposes an open mouth." She studied me with sad disdain, in my muddied elbows, and blue jeans grass-stained. She spoke into the chasm between my legs. "If only God had spared a bit more dough. If only he had made you a boy," my mother said. She slapped my knees together and simmered. She lit a cigarette and exhaled. She stared into the sun and squinted. She looked at her hand on the window, at her fingerprints in the dust, at her fist against the pane. She looked at the black boys with boom boxes, the asphalt with homeless men, the buses hissing beneath our building. And then she returned to her own reflection. She studied it from all sorts of angles, a dull object, a sharp blade. "If I didn't love you so much," she said, "this face could still take me away from here."

BETTY NOBUE KANO
DEDICATION

Yuri Kochiyama, activist; Arundhati Roy, writer; and Maya Lin, architect

Yuri Kochiyama: for her intense spirit of social justice she changes the course of history. She is a political leader, activist, mother, grandmother, great-grandmother, godmother and founder of numerous social justice organizations supporting political prisoners, anti-apartheid, Puerto Rican liberation, etc. At eighty-five she is demonstrating with today's youth taking their struggle to the streets and the courtrooms. Arundhati Roy: author of the Booker Prize–winning *God of Small Things*. The South Asian internationalist living in New Delhi, India is an awesome political thinker and leader. With wit, forceful intelligence, an economy of words, generosity of spirit and relentless courage she brings clarity, purpose and analysis to today's troubled times. Maya Lin: for her memorable, quietly "earth-shattering" Vietnam Veterans Memorial that remains a hallmark of a profound and commanding memorial. She has written a page in public art that is all her own and inspires many.

BETTY NOBUE KANO
Ogun. Acrylic on canvas, 36" x 30"

ANH-HOA THI NGUYEN
DEDICATION

Trinh T. Minh-Ha, filmmaker, writer, professor

She revealed the beauty of my name during her "Women in Film" class at U.C. Berkeley. She pronounced my name as a song, in proper sequence, traditional to Vietnamese culture. She called Nguyen Thi Anh-Hoa. I barely recognized the tones and rhythms, the poetry that belongs to me. In my twenties, I admired Trinh T. Minh-Ha as the only Vietnamese woman professor I knew and for her astounding intellect and vision. Years later, I heard her read a poem in French from her book, *en minuscules* about a Buddhist monk that set himself on fire. The poem *Par Amour Pour Autrui* amazed me, not only for its breathtaking quality, but previously, I had conceptualized my own poem, *A Buddhist Heart*, inspired by the same Vietnamese monk. Trinh T. Minh-Ha influences my writing and visual art through her poetry and compelling contributions to feminist theory, post-colonial studies, cinema and literature.

A BUDDHIST HEART
ANH-HOA THI NGUYEN

Each time I burned my body for you, my heart remained intact—a lotus perfumed in gasoline sacrificed at your feet. I watched the saffron flames engulf me, watched them sear away my skin, crimson flesh of a plum stripped of its peel. Tender and glowing like Mars, I would rise to the sky for you to see me. In those moments I was your torch and we were united. United by the gaze, the scent, the heat, the shutter. For love of another, I'd whisper to myself, faithful in muted pain. My hope, my heart, extinguishing as you stand there, paralyzed, each time, like a still camera unable to look away.

VANESSA MERINA
DEDICATION

M. Evelina Galang, writer

I can tell you exactly where I was when I read my first M. Evelina Galang story. I was standing in line at the Torrance, California DMV and a woman in front of me was holding a copy of Galang's *Her Wild American Self*. I was startled to see "wild" and "American" against a sea of brown faces that looked like mine. Galang was the first Filipina American writer I discovered and she continues to be a thinker I return to. She is lyrical, brutal in her descriptions of racial and sexual stereotypes, unafraid to write with the intent of effecting social change. Through her stories, and later her essays and novel, *One Tribe*, I found a literary role model who challenged me to think about what we owe to our communities as writers and how we can help bring the voices of traditionally silenced peoples to light. Galang's writing spans not just generations and geographies, but genres, proving that one doesn't have to limit herself to fiction or non-fiction, that everything is up for grabs. Beyond that, she is a writing instructor with an appreciation for craft that rivals her need to uncover truth. Writing, Galang has said, "is how I make sense of the world around me." Yes, I say. And thank you.

THE BOY WITH A SWITCH IN HIS BACK
VANESSA MERINA

The children didn't believe that Thomas had a real on/off switch until, one rainy Wednesday, when the class was bidden by Miss Blackwell to stay inside the classroom for lunch, he lifted his t-shirt and showed them.

The switch looked tough and small. It stood upright in the "on" position, a metallic nub sprouting from the soft flesh between the boy's shoulder blades. The students forgot their bag lunches on their desks. They glanced at their teacher who sat in one corner of the room correcting spelling tests, and drew closer to Thomas as he stood beside the blue bookcase.

"Is it—" Rose Hodgkinson began.

"—real?" finished Thomas. "Yeah."

"And can we—" she stepped tentatively forward.

"No," said Thomas more sharply than the children liked. "Please don't."

From the beginning, Thomas had reminded them of an animal who'd been shuttled to their school from some far-off place, like the pacing panthers or plumed birds at the zoo. He was quiet, with features that seemed pieced together from different lands. He used words the children thought strange and beautiful with meanings that were lost to Miss Blackwell.

Thomas said very little, and when he did speak it was because he'd been addressed. The one exception to this was his quiet jabber during the flag salute each morning. Even after Miss Blackwell sent him to the corner of the room for refusing to participate, Thomas continued his murmuring in a measured, almost musical, whisper.

Once, Miss Blackwell had explained to the class that many of the words that Thomas used were nonsense. When several of the children shook their heads, the teacher's face reddened and she put her hands on her hips.

"For example," she said, "I challenge you to find vorlandoolious in the dictionary. It simply doesn't exist."

The children jumped from their chairs, grabbed the big, red

dictionaries off the shelves and pried them open. They huddled two to a book because there weren't enough to go around, their fingers dancing over the pages in search of Thomas' word.

"Or maralalara," pronounced Miss Blackwell as the children searched. "I dare you to find *that* one."

The students tried hard to locate the words but came up only with entries that sounded vaguely similar: vomitus, voracious, vorticella. For maralalara, which the children especially liked, they could find only maraca, maraschino, marathon.

Reluctantly, they concluded that their teacher must be right. There were sighs as the dictionaries were returned to the shelves. Several students avoided Thomas' eyes for fear he'd see their disappointment. But Thomas simply smiled and nodded his head as the three o'clock bell rang to signal the end of the day, and the children filed out the door to be collected by their parents.

Although it wasn't his intention, Thomas was disquieting. He mostly played alone and was the last in line when the children gathered to go to recess or to the cafeteria for lunch. He seemed uninterested in the cliques that formed daily, the struggle between the stronger and weaker students, the talk of birthdays and playovers. Yet he was seduced by the lessons and, as though his life depended on it, Thomas never gave an incorrect answer to a question. Whether it was memorizing state capitals or locating the missing glue bottles for an art project, Thomas was always, incorrigibly, right.

Now, as the children drew nearer, Thomas stood still, his face watchful.

"Does it hurt?" asked Melissa, frowning with concern and touching her own back through her grass-colored dress.

"No," said Thomas.

"Were you born like that?" asked Daniel. He imagined his baby sister, Claire—barely two months old—with a switch that he could snap to stop her wailing. He'd watched his mother bathe Claire, though, and seen nothing but pink skin.

"I guess so," said Thomas. Sensing his classmates' confusion, he tried to describe what it felt like. "It's like another ear or nose but it's deeper, like a plant root," he stumbled.

The children waited for him to say more. They realized that at this close distance they could make out a slight hum deep within the dark-haired boy. The sound, faint and steady, made them think of their refrigerators at home or the soft rumble of their parents' cars.

Seth, the tallest boy in class, grabbed playfully at Thomas' back. "So what's it do besides turn off and on?" he asked.

The other students snickered nervously. They knew that Seth was drawn to any new toy that wasn't his.

"That's all," Thomas answered. "It just turns off and on. But that's a lot."

"So what happens if I…" Seth threw his hands at Thomas and the smaller boy jumped and ducked away. The children's eyes grew big and no one moved until Seth laughed. "Just kidding," he said.

"Please don't touch," Thomas said. This seemed very important to him.

"What's going on here?" Miss Blackwell was suddenly standing above the small gathering. She'd approached from her desk several yards away and was frowning, still holding a few spelling tests in her right hand.

No one answered. Thomas pulled down his shirt and turned to face the teacher.

"Thomas, what's going on?" Miss Blackwell tried again. She shook the spelling tests which rattled dryly. Red pen marks covered the papers and Anna, seeing her name on one of them, started to cry.

"Anna, please." Miss Blackwell said. She addressed the class, "Apparently you're using your lunch period for show and tell. Well, I hope you've gotten it out of your system. Please go grab your lunches."

The children did as they were told. They had just begun eating when Thomas beckoned them to the bookcase, and now the sight of food made their stomachs growl.

"Take your lunches and bring them to me," Miss Blackwell instructed.

The children did so. Miss Blackwell produced a plastic garbage pail from behind her desk. "Now throw them away."

The children paused, their lunches in their hands.

"Teacher?" a few of them asked.

"Throw them away," Miss Blackwell repeated. "And please thank Thomas for making you go hungry today."

One by one, the students approached the pail and threw away their uneaten lunches. They looked at Miss Blackwell, then at Thomas. Thomas stared back, his face impenetrable. As always, he was the last to rise and join the line, the last to throw away his lunch. It rested on top of the other paper bags, an open juice box tipping partly out. As Thomas crossed the front of the room to return to his desk, Miss Blackwell raised her hand.

"Stop," she said. She put the now-full garbage back behind her desk and stood, smoothing out her skirt. Then she walked to the chalkboard, took up a piece of chalk and drew a small white circle on the board.

"What's this?" Miss Blackwell asked the class.

"An egg?" Andra offered from the back of the room. She'd had an egg in her lunch, a hardboiled one.

"A cookie," Ian guessed.

Miss Blackwell shook her head. "No, it's a circle that Thomas will put his nose against for the rest of the day."

The children hoped he'd put up a fight, even a small one, but Thomas stuck his nose against the green board, his back to the class. The faint outline of the switch was visible beneath his t-shirt.

The day resumed.

By one o'clock the drizzle outside had become a downpour. Great sheets threw themselves against the back windows and Miss Blackwell, giving a lesson on the early Spanish missions, had to get up and close the classroom door to be heard. The children followed the lesson in their history books as best they could, looking up every now and then at Thomas, then back down at the pages in front of them. With aching stomachs they began to pay close attention to the descriptions of the missions' meals and crops, the neat rows of squash and berries, the fragrant mint and rosemary that grew on steps in pots.

Seth wrote a note on paper torn from his textbook demanding gum. The children passed the note from row to row, sliding it with their shoes to one another, or tossing it underhand when Miss Blackwell turned her back to write something on the board. The request produced three cinnamon jelly beans and a stick of winterfresh gum that Seth chewed with his mouth open, not sharing. When April Frye scowled at him, he stuck out a bright red tongue.

At two o'clock it was time for math, but the children were having trouble concentrating. They stared at Thomas' back, their faces pale, and wouldn't look at Miss Blackwell when called upon. Charlie Hart, usually strong in math, wrongly answered three questions in a row and was bordering on tears. He stared up at Miss Blackwell, then turned to the class and then to Thomas who stood with his nose to the egg-cookie-circle.

"Hungry?" Miss Blackwell asked, smiling.

Charlie nodded.

"It's very hard to concentrate when you're hungry," observed Miss Blackwell. She faced the class. "Charlie in particular is finding it hard to concentrate."

Outside, the rain bore down, drumming loudly on the windows and against the door. Miss Blackwell allowed the children time to listen to the rain and to Charlie's quiet sniffling. With a little whistle in her nose, she sighed and began to erase the math problems from the board, implying they'd find no right answer today.

"Wait—" Charlie Hart was out of his chair. He ignored Miss Blackwell's commands to sit down, and walked from his desk to the place where Thomas stood at the front of the class with his nose to the blackboard.

"You know the answer?" he asked Thomas, quietly at first, then with growing impatience. "You know the answer, don't you?" Charlie wiped his wet eyes with the back of his hand.

Thomas nodded, not moving from the board.

"What is it?" spat Charlie.

Thomas seemed to hesitate, his shoulders quaking slightly. "Twenty-two and a third," he said softly, so only a handful of people heard.

Charlie stood staring, his mouth fixed in a rigid line. Then, in one quick movement, he yanked up Thomas' t-shirt to reveal the switch.

• • •

After that I'm afraid our story becomes fiction, because I can't be wholly sure of what happened next. Even when my nieces and nephews come to visit and beg me to tell the story of Thomas, pleading, "Auntie Rose, what happened to little Thomas?" their eyes filling with a hard light, I can't be sure I'm relaying justly what took place. I have told the story a dozen times and each time the details shift. My memory isn't what it used to be, and I have to concentrate to recall the angle of the daylight through the classroom windows, the high whistle of Miss Blackwell's rheumatic nose.

And yet I remember the rain: the steady thrash commanding us forward as we walked out into it toward the water-blackened playground and, without speaking a word, trooped into a circle just the way we had earlier in the day beside the blue bookcase.

Someone—I'm not sure if it was Miss Blackwell, but I do remember the clicking of her heels against the pavement—brought Thomas, for once at the front of the line, to the center of our circle where he stood, looking smaller and wetter than the rest of us. His t-shirt was pulled up to his armpits and his skin was pimpled from the cold. The switch, still turned to "on," glinted feebly. We laughed despite ourselves—a high, nervous sound—

that seemed to fly out and be eaten by the wind. Thomas stood at the center, wilting. He didn't try to run, he didn't move from his spot.

There was a feeling of inevitability, and of time running out. It would be a matter of minutes before the other teachers, in the midst of their lessons, peered out the window and wondered why we were there, why we'd been allowed outside. Or before our parents, arriving early to pick up younger siblings, exited their cars to see what was going on. And so Seth, though it could have been any one of us, walked up to Thomas as he stood shivering and turned the switch to "off."

There was a high-pitched pop and then a complicated mix of thumps and hisses, of parts chugging slowly to a stop. By this time, Thomas' face was turned upwards toward the sky as though he wanted to see where so much rain was coming from, and how it could be so steady and so strong.

We stood and watched him like that for another minute, his small face turned skyward, eyes and nostrils filling up with water until small seizures coursed through his body and we were fully sure. And then we turned and we fell in line like we'd been taught and we walked back to the classroom where it was warm and safe and dry.

CLARA HSU
DEDICATION

*Noemi Sohn, Filipina American feminist
with cerebral palsy, poet, activist, educator,
friend*

Your sensuality defines femininity.
Your boldness the crown
of fierce honesty.
Your spirit boundless
in a world of narrow vision.

May your voice be heard
so the oppressed, the disabled, the neglected
shall manifest their existence
as the fabric of humanity.

THE CALL
CLARA HSU

Waxen moon
in greasy wok
simmering over black coal.
Fertility blessing
reddens wall
in chamber of draped bed.

Tighten the binding
on your breasts,
your feet,
ignore the wind,
the fluttering of wings.
In a thousand days
you will become
a proper woman.

Come, sisters,
strike your drums,
over waves we glide.
Skip a frenzied dance
on freezing water,
brush azure rain,
splatter on rice paper sky.

There, toward the rising sun
you lift your veil
and shed your garments.
Wild-step under ancient trees,
dash rainbow
among blades of grass.

At midnight we spill
star dust, stir dreams,
lilt with winking fireflies,
emerge from silver light
aglow.

Contributors

Melba Abela is an interdisciplinary artist and writer currently living and working in San Francisco. Her works have been shown nationally and in the Philippines and have been published in arts and literary journals.

Terry Acebo Davis is a visual artist whose work has been exhibited nationally and internationally. Her installations use printmaking to build tableaux works that draw upon her travels, history and identity as a Pilipina Amerikan.

Susan Almazol is a sculptor, writer and educator. Using sculpture to express multiple realities, Susan aims to draw the viewer into a tantalizing dialogue of what is the real deal.

M. Grace Ilagan Angel is a painter, poet and photographer. Married, with two beautiful and artistic girls, she is an event planner and arts fundraiser. Her works have been exhibited in the Bay Area and internationally. Grace is currently working on a collection of poems entitled *From a Fanatic Heart*.

Katherine Aoki received her MFA in printmaking from Washington University in St. Louis in 1994. She creates narrative prints, paintings and sculpture that address gender issues. Her artwork is regularly exhibited at local, national and international venues. Aoki is currently an assistant professor of art at Santa Clara University.

Tamiko Beyer's poetry has appeared or is forthcoming in numerous journals, including *Calyx*, *Crab Creek Review*, *Mizna*, *Gay and Lesbian Review* and *Triplopia*. She is a Kundiman Asian American Poet Fellow and she leads writing workshops for homeless LGBT youth through the New York Writers Coalition.

Olivia Boler's first novel, *Year of the Smoke Girl*, was published in 2000 by Dry Bones Press. A freelance writer, Boler has published in *Mary*, *Hyphen*, and *San Francisco Chronicle Book Review*, among others. She lives in her native San Francisco, and can be reached through her website, www.oliviaboler.com.

Ann Carli's short stories have appeared in *APAJ*, *Pearl* and *Gentle Strength Quarterly*. She considers her day job, as an independent feature film producer, creative midwifery. In 1999 she was awarded a Golden Ring Award